CCCM - User's Progress.mht

A PHYSICIAN'S

PRESCRIPTION FOR

SUCCESSFUL INVESTING

By

Jacob I. Haft, MD

An investment guide for professionals, and others, who are smart, busy, have a modest amount of Discretionary Capital and don't have the time to do the research.

Third Edition

Published by Lulu.com, Raleigh, NC

This book was printed in the United States of America

ISBN 978-1-387-23759-9

Brief note by the author and why this book was written:

For many years I was privileged to be chief of cardiology at a teaching hospital in New Jersey.   During that time, in addition to practicing medicine I had the opportunity to teach numerous medical students, interns and residents and to train a number of cardiology fellows—the best and the brightest culled from the medical house staff—who worked very closely with me.   When they first began they considered me to be the fount of infallible wisdom.   As they matured they realized this was not necessarily true, but even after they finished training and have established successful careers in practice and in academia, they have continued to call on me for advice in managing difficult cases.   As time has gone on the advice they have wanted has been less medical and more political, personal, and career related. More recently, the advice they have sought has been more economic.

Over the years I have been fairly successful in investing and playing the markets.   I have developed a number of algorithms and techniques that work for me and that have worked for a number of my friends and associates.

In answer to my former fellows who have asked me how I do it, I have written this small book. Most busy people, like my former trainees, have a relatively short attention span so I have endeavored to keep the chapters short and to the point.

In early 2009 I added a fairly long addendum chapter that gives my take on the 2007-2009 economic debacle. I have re-edited the book in 2017 and have updated some of the data on newsletters and have added a second addendum chapter to deal with the current status of the economy. My suggestions on what to do now may be of especial interest.

I hope this book will be useful to novice investors and also to all those who want a guide to attain financial security but don't have the time to work at it.

.

Table of Contents

Chapter 1: How I Learned To Invest

I learned to invest from three sources:

#1---My Father.

#2---Gambling in College

#3---My First Secretary when I Switched Jobs

My father was an intelligent, incurable optimist. He was a gambler and loved this country. He came to the U.S. in 1912 when he was eighteen years old, and landed in Galveston, Texas. He left his first job after 3 days because he felt exploited. Though he spoke no English, he sold bananas off of a horse and wagon, at 10 cents a pound, 3 pounds a quarter. He later became the owner of a haberdashery business and then a jewelry store. He left these to wander up the Texas panhandle during the oil rush, in the Red River Valley. He started his own oil company (Rose 88) in Oklahoma. The oil field was shallow and the wells went dry. The Red River changed its course and his oil contracts changed states and were ultimately tied up in litigation. He lost everything.

He then traveled around Texas buying scrap metal (unused rail lines) for a junk yard he owned in Houston. He sold the junk yard and was thereafter recruited by a few San Antonio businessmen to open up a dormant silver mine in Mexico. He opened the mine and became the "patrone" of a small town. I still have receipts he kept for ore, from the American Smelting Company (subsequently Asarco) from the early 1920's. The mine was a financial success. His salary and profits were paid in shares.

In the 1920's, there was great political ferment in Mexico and bands of armed revolutionaries roamed the countryside. One night, around 1925, the townspeople, who apparently liked and respected my father, came to his house and told him he must leave immediately. He did. The following day, Zapata, one of the more ruthless revolutionary leaders, and his men came to town, killed all the gringos (nonMexicans) and subsequently all natural resources, including silver, were nationalized. My father lost everything---again.

He returned to Texas and wandered around Texas for a while. He drove to California in a model T, and eventually arrived in New York. He leased and ran a butter and eggs concession in a big grocery store for a while, but this form of work did not suit him.

In 1931 he heard of the possibility of a job selling life insurance in Newark, New Jersey. When the recruiter heard his foreign accent he was rejected immediately; he challenged the recruiter that if he sold three policies in two hours, he would get the job. He sold three policies in one hour and got the job. He subsequently married my mother and over the next six years, my sister and I were born.

My father had been a rich man a few times, and had lost it all each time. He became a successful insurance agent because he was personable, honest, very intelligent, and knowledgeable. To many of the people to whom he sold life insurance, and whom he visited to collect premiums, he became a family friend and a trusted financial advisor.   The majority of them were immigrants, like him, and he helped them with their mortgages, banking and debts.

He enjoyed the insurance business because he was free to come and go as he pleased. He went to the horse races whenever he wanted (he owned a racehorse at one time—

Starshine), he played cards all night on occasion, and he hung out at a friend's real estate agency, and at another friend's brokerage house.

I often rode with him in his old Chrysler after school when he made his rounds to collect insurance premiums.   He talked about whatever was on his mind.   He gave me arithmetic problems to solve; he taught me about the stock market, and talked of his current investments.   He was interested in getting rich quick, and had many penny stocks in gold mines, uranium mines, and sulfur mines.   He bought Skyatron, a cable TV Company, well before its time and had many other "story" stocks.

From what he told me and by how he invested, it appeared that he had certain principles:

1.   Buy only round lots (100 shares and multiples thereof)—never odd lots.

2.   Get an idea and if you believe in it, commit all your resources to it and stick to it through thick and thin.

3.   Never sell a loser; it will come back, have faith.

4.   Never buy a stock that pays a dividend. They are for widows and orphans and never go up much. They are not reinvesting their profits.

My father always lost money on the stock exchange, though he did well as a salesman.   Our family was well provided for and we had everything we needed.   He was especially concerned that my sister and I received an excellent education. He had a few real estate investments that allowed my mother to live fairly well for twenty years after his death without requiring any assistance from my sister or from me.

Because he wanted to get rich quick and loved story stocks to which he was very loyal, never selling them as they went down, loved no-dividend stocks, which he felt would grow faster, cheap stocks that he thought would go up faster and round lots, never buying less than 100 shares at a time, he was a very unsuccessful stock investor.

I realized this very early on and learned the following, which has worked very well for me:

1.   Don't worry about round lots (multiples of 100).   Buy good stocks no matter the price.   Buying one share of Berkeshire Hathaway or 30 shares of IBM is usually a better investment than buying 3000 shares of most stocks that sell for $1.00. The odd lot fee, which used to be high, no longer exists.

2.   If you are wrong, admit it and cut your losses.   Set a loss level that is not catastrophic.   For example, 30 percent.   Sell if you've made a mistake.

3.   Invest as if you are a widow or an orphan. Much of your investment capital should be in dividend producing stocks. The presence of a dividend usually means that the company is producing a product, or a service for which there is a market, that is being successfully sold.   That company, more often than not, is generating a profit. With dividends, you can sit on a stock even if it has a period of slow, or no appreciation.   In addition, over the long run, even in systems not as good as mine, stocks generate 9-10 per cent per year; 3 per cent to 5 per cent of that is dividends.

4.   Never put all your investment capital into one stock, or even one sector of the market, no matter how sure you are that it will go up   You may be wrong and you can quickly lose a lot. Tips and "inside" information are notorious traps for even the seasoned investor.   Diversify.   Get many ideas and put small amounts in each.   Over the long run you will do better.

The next source of investment wisdom came from some modest gambling experiences in college.

Every January and every May, we had at Harvard what was called a "reading period". A few weeks before exams started, there were no classes. Students were frequently assigned a few additional readings but the main purpose of the reading period was to allow us to study for finals at whatever individual rhythm was effective without interruption to attend classes.

Studying gets boring.

One reading period, my roommate and I---he was a near mathematical genius-- decided to break the tedium by playing the horses. We had a system. Every morning we bought the Armstrong Daily, a tout sheet (that may not exist now) that listed all the races in the country, The sheet picked three favorites in each race. The sheet's record was about 30-35% correct. We did a dry run on the sheet without betting money, and found that these percentages of correct winner-picking were fairly consistent. We played the daily double at each of three racetracks. To win the daily double we must pick the winning horse in the first two races. A winning $2.00 bet on the daily double would usually pay $18 to $24, that is, 9-12 to one. We figured the odds of the sheet picking a winner in each race was about one in three. If we played the favorites of the first 2 races our chance of winning was 1 in 9 (1/3 times 1/3). If we played the favorite in the first race and place horse pick--the one favored to come in second who very often came in first--- in the second race; and a third bet on the second favorite in the first race and the favorite in the second race, our odds of winning the daily double were approximately one in three (1/9+1/9+1/9). If we followed the same procedure at three tracks, we should win at least one daily double from the 9 bets. Since the payoff was usually 9 to 1, or better, we figured we should end up ahead.

After we read the Armstrong Daily during our midmorning study break, my roommate called his friend at Tufts, who would relay the picks to his bookie. We had given him $30 each so we had a pool to play with. We would get the results on the radio at about 6:00 PM each day.

During the reading period and into the exam period, we bet $18/day (9 bets). Most days we won at least one daily double and most winnings were greater than $18; not by much. At the end of the exam period we were each up about $30. We took back our initial investment, and because we had to go back to classes, we blew the $60 on a few bets that were out of the system and lost it all. What did I learn?

1. Buy good advice and follow it. Most good advice is correct about 35% of the time. Otherwise the advisor goes out of business.

2. Use a system (a discipline) that works and stick to it. If you arbitrarily leave it you will probably lose.

3. Diversify. Use the advice but assume it will *not* be correct all the time. You do not know when it will be correct so try all the suggestions.

My secretary:

When I moved to the position I subsequently held for 24 years, I inherited a secretary and two typists. The secretary did not like the fact that I had replaced the former chief to whom she was loyal. It was obvious she was not going to be an asset. I let her remain as head of the secretarial pool but looked for a new secretary. The Chief of Medicine suggested H. H's husband, who had been Chief of Obstetrics and Gynecology, had died of cancer at 47 years old about a year before. She was bored and looking for a job. The problem was, she had four children, the youngest was still in high school, and she had to be home by 3:30 PM. She was bright, personable, with superb secretarial skills. She was familiar with the politics of the hospital and knew all of the personalities. I hired her. It was one of the best decisions I ever made. She was loyal, exceedingly helpful, and made my transition into the new position and into the new culture easy.

H was also very rich. She inherited money from her husband, and from his insurance. She had to invest it. She visited a number of investment symposia and told me about them. She also shared audio tapes that they gave out. I listened to them. She came to the conclusion that the best way to learn to invest and the best way to get investment ideas, was to subscribe to investment letters. She showed me the letters and I was impressed. The first letter we used was the Jim Dines letter ---- which still exists--- and another, John Dessauers letter, that no longer exists. We profited from the letters. Subsequently H's kids grew up, she remarried and moved away and sadly, had to leave me.

Over the years I have used many letters. Of ten stocks they pick, typically, three (like the Armstrong Daily) are excellent and go up by 50-150%, 2 stocks go down by greater than 50% and 5 stocks go up or down by 10-20% or stay the same. The difference from the racing form, however, is that the winners clearly make up for the losers, and, moreover you can get rid of the losers before the losses become excessive by using a mental stop loss discipline. More on this later.

The trick is to find the letters that have this ratio or better. The best letter I ever used was the Ruta letter—he was very right about 70% of the time (the stocks went up substantially) and only about 10% wrong (the stocks plummeted).. Unfortunately, he died and his successor could not keep it up and the letter was discontinued.

Hence, from my secretary I learned:

1. There is a universe of excellent investment newsletters.

And reinforced:

2. Buy good advice and follow it.

Chapter 2:   First, The Things NOT To Do.

Very Bad Advice #1:   Only buy round lots. I.e., 100 or more shares; do not buy odd lots.

Very Bad Advice #2:   Stocks that pay dividends are for widows and orphans. Buy only stocks that keep all their profits to fuel "growth".

Very Bad Advice #3:   Buy only stocks in small companies—they appreciate faster. Avoid stocks in big stable blue chips, they are for wimps.

Very Bad advice #4:   Make up your mind and go with your convictions and invest a lot in a few stocks. You will make it big when you guess right.

Very Bad Advice #5:   You are as smart, or smarter, than the Wall Street gang.

Very Bad Advice #6:   Use a broker with a big firm. He has excellent resources and advice.   He always has your best interests at heart.

Very Bad Advice #7: Always buy the new funds and other investment instruments concocted by big brokerage firms; e.g. a China Fund or a Growth Fund.

Very Bad Advice #8: Don't worry about commissions.   Your broker is worth it.

Very Bad Advice #9:   Invest only in Big name mutual funds.
Their managers know the market and will do best by you.   Forget
individual stocks.

Very Bad Advice #10:   Time the market.   Get out when it is bad
and get in when it has gone up.

Very Bad Advice #11:   Never take a loss. If you hold on long
enough it will go up again.

Very Bad Advice #12:   Follow hot stories and hot stocks, that's
where the money is.

Very bad Advice #13:   Always take profits as soon as they
appear, or God will take them away.

Very Bad Advice #14:   The idea is to turn over stocks as quickly
as possible.   Long term holdings are for unimaginative wimps.

Very Bad Advice #15:   Your friends at the country club or at the
cocktail party really know what's going on: always follow their hot
tips.

Very Bad Advice #16:   Hot tips and inside information are how to get rich.

Very Bad Advice #17:   Don't ever average down.

Very Bad Advice #18:   Don't buy stocks after they have gone up.

Very Bad Advice #19:   Commit yourself to whatever stock you believe in and be loyal.   Hold it through thick and thin.

Very Bad Advice #20:   Your brother-in-law, uncle, cousin, best friend, the Accountant, the stock broker, lawyer, bank teller, knows much more than you do. Always follow his advice.

Very Bad Advice #21:   If you *know* something is good, bet the farm and go for broke.

Very Bad Advice #22:   Options are the best way to make it big.

Very Bad Advice #23:   Futures are great and playing the futures proves you have very big ones and you will eventually be very rich.

Very Bad Advice #24:   Never pay for advice. Financial newsletters you pay for are for suckers.   There is plenty of excellent free advice on the internet, in your mail box and from your stock broker.

Very Bad Advice #25:   When using a newsletter you are paying for, do your own research because you are smarter than the newsletter writer, and really can pick and choose which will go up among his recommendations.

Chapter 3:   While Standing On One Foot ---The Essence of This Book

1) Diversify—never commit yourself to one stock or one sector

2) Buy advice and follow it—buy market newsletters.

3) Have a "chip" and commit only one chip at a time.   For example, $800, $1,000, $2,000, $3,000, $4,000, $5,000. Buy that

amount of a stock whether 1 share, 7 shares, 15 shares, 42 shares, 100 shares,120 shares, 200, 300, 500, or 2000 shares at a time. Do not fear odd lots.

4) Follow your success by the bottom line—the total value of the portfolio, not of individual stocks.

5) Get a discount brokerage account—preferably one with a human you can talk to. It can be a different person each time. There are fewer errors than in a fully computerized account. Don't pay large commissions.

6) Set a sale point with a mental stop—do not put in stop orders except for stocks on the NY Stock exchange and even then, far away from the buy-in price. For instance 25-35 per cent. Don't be reluctant to cut your losses.

7) You may want one account in a full service brokerage firm (with high commissions). Consider Merrill Lynch, Morgan Stanley, UBS, Wells Fargo, etcetera, because they will help with specialized accounts such as retirement, IRAs, or Education Accounts. But always have a discount account where most of your investments should be.

8) Have a separate discount account which is *not* a margin account in which you invest in stocks that pay more than 3-4 per cent dividends. Have the dividends sent to you once or twice a month. This account may best be in your spouse's

name. He or she will enjoy the little "gifts" every month and will not yell about your investing. That's at least 3 accounts.

9) When in doubt, buy industrial (not utilities) stocks listed on the NYSE that pay 3-4.5% dividends, and that produce products, or services, for which there is a demand that will probably be in business ten years from the time of purchase.

10)   See the last third of the Addendum chapter and the second addendum chapter for specific advice on how to deal with the current economy and market turbulence.

Remember, you only have to get rich once, so slow and steady ---moderately conservative--- does it best, cutting losses and riding winners most of the time.

Chapter 4: General Financial Advice

Before starting an aggressive investment strategy, there are a few general principles you should follow before considering that you have discretionary capital to invest.

1. Get life insurance, especially if you have a wife and children.

Physicians; buy term insurance that you can get through organizations that you belong to; for example, the local medical society, the AMA, the specialty society you belong to, such as the American College of Physicians, Chest Physicians, Cardiology, etcetera. You should have at least $1 million--- that is relatively inexpensive, depending on your age. If you are salaried, consider regular life insurance; it costs more but you automatically build up a nest egg you can turn to in emergencies.

2. Make sure you have good health insurance. If you take a big deductible, the rates are more reasonable; what you really want is catastrophic insurance.
A prescription plan is also necessary, again with a big deductible. Anticancer drugs and drugs such as the biologicals and immunopharmaceuticals, and the novel antiarthritis drugs can be very expensive.

3. Have disability insurance. Your main asset is your health. If you can't work, you have no income; especially if you run a small business or are in solo private practice. You must service your overhead, whether you work or not.

Physicians: If you are early in private practice there is a delay between starting practice and the first insurance or Medicare reimbursement checks. Use the first checks, before you become accustomed to living more affluently, to pay off your debts, especially the debts associated with equipment purchases.   The interest rates are high and make up a significant amount of your monthly "nut"—payments that must be made every month. Try to lower your overhead as much as possible. Hold off on buying the fancy car. The old one can work for another year. There is no rush to pay off your student loans; the interest rates are usually reasonable. And, of course, you should have no credit card debt. Card balances should always be paid off first. No one can consistently get more than 15-24% compounded monthly, the usual credit card rate, from any investment that is available.   The rates are probably not worse from the local entrepreneur, the one who goes after your kneecaps if you don't pay.

4. Always have cash or a CD reserve of at least 3 months of living and overhead expenses on hand, and hope you never need it.

5.   Set up a retirement account—early—using pretax dollars. They can grow rapidly. This should be with a regular broker and you should pick the stocks—no mutual funds.   No stocks in this account should be speculative. They should be large cap stocks, and all should pay dividends of 2.5 to 4.5 per cent. (Regular IRA's, 401 accounts or 401B accounts are using pre-tax dollars—you pay taxes at the earned income rate when you draw out the original money and the tax free appreciation when you retire. The expectation is that you will be in a lower income tax bracket when you retire and the amount of taxes you will pay will be much less than the amount you pay when you are working. However this is not always the case, because of the usual constant inflation. There is another type of IRA, a Roth IRA. This is funded with after-tax money. However, the money drawnout, after retirement including any appreciation on the original money is tax-free when it is withdrawn. If you feel you will be in a higher tax bracket when you retire, a Roth account might be a better alternative. If possible you should consider having 2 IRAs, a Roth and a regular IRA.

6.   Consider an educational IRA (526) if you have young children. The money invested in such an account is after-tax;

but any appreciation or dividends are not taxed.   This also
should be a conservative account.

Chapter 5: Getting Started—Picking a Broker

1)   Do *not* use a financial advisor.   Typically he will charge an upfront fee and then a yearly percentage of your total assets, usually 2-5 per cent of your account, depending on the value of your account.   If you consider that under his tutelage your account will grow 9-11% per year, if he is knowledgeable, (he will promise much more and show you an account he has handled that has appreciated at a higher percentage in the past 2 or 3 years; ask him to show you five accounts, and see the average appreciation). This 2-5 per cent is 1/5 to ½ the yearly account appreciation.   Moreover, he will steer you to vendors with whom he has a deal, such as insurance salesmen, that you should not use since you are getting probably the best available rates through organizations you belong to, and to stockbrokers who charge higher commissions so they can pay him his cut.

More importantly, since he benefits greatly if you make an unexpected large profit and loses little if you take a large loss, he has an incentive to take chances with your money. In addition, if your total asset value goes down because some of his ideas did not work out, he will lose interest in your account since the value of his percentage will decrease, and it is unlikely that you will give him a good recommendation. When you need him the most he will be unreachable and will exert little effort on your behalf. If you follow our methods you will not need or benefit further by using an investment advisor.

2)   You should have at least two accounts. Your main account should be with a discount broker; E-Trade, Fidelity, Ameritrade or another firm that charges less than $25 per trade (a buy or sell event) usually <$15. And you should have a second account with a full service broker such as Morgan Stanley, Merrill Lynch, Wells Fargo or UBS. Use your full service broker to help you set up an IRA, Roth and other specialized retirement or other accounts you may need as the years go by; don't use an expensive full service firm for most of your trading and investing. Never depend on the advice of this stock broker. The stocks that he will tout are only those that are suggested by the brokerage firm. Typically they are stocks

that have recently had a run up and hence are "not speculative".
Usually they do not continue to run after they are bought; they
stay the same or go down. They are generally safe and
conventional, so the brokerage firm has no chance of being sued
for giving inappropriate advice, even if the stocks plummet.

    Also, under no circumstances buy funds designed by the
big brokerage firm to follow a hot sector. The formation of
these funds are a sign that a winning run is at an end and the
stocks in the sector are about of go down. I saw this in the first
China bull market in the early 1990's. When Merrill came out
with an in-house China fund it was at their peak. The fund
rapidly plummeted, and losses were great.   The same thing
happened in the late 1990's.   Smith Barney came out with an
in-house technology fund just at the peak of the dot-com bubble.
If one were to be cynical, one could suggest that these funds are
set up so the brokerage house has a vehicle to which they can
sell these soon-to-be super losers from favored managed
accounts. They can sell large numbers of these shares to new
funds at the current market price without going through the
market.   If they sold large volumes of soon-to-be-dog stocks
through the usual market place, the value of these stocks would
go down because there are few real buyers.   By selling them
to a fund without going through a public market, they avoid

"disrupting" the market which would happen if they sold such large amounts of these stocks in the wide open auction market (which are what the New York, American, Nasdaq and foreign exchanges really are) where they would only sell at a reasonable price.

And for this type of advice the buyer pays premium commissions. The minimal commission for the usual retail customers is $90-$150 per trade.   If you buy stock in blocks of $1000 to $5000 (to have a diversified portfolio) this amounts to 3-10% of the stocks value, which is usually more than a years-worth of dividends and eats up about 1/3 to ½ of a years' stock appreciation.

Also be alert to the fact that new stocks and other investment vehicles pushed by full service brokers usually entail commissions about twice the commission of a stock bought through the usual exchange.   These costs are easily seen in the prospectus: For example, in the offering prospectus they will clearly state that of the million dollars raised in the initial stock offering $50,000, (5%) or more will go for "underwriting costs" and only $950,000 will go to the company.   If you try to sell the vehicle within one month you will get back about 80-85 per cent of your initial cost if you are lucky.   The small retail investor never gets a piece of a hot initial public offering (IPO), only the IPO's that no one wants, and post marketing of the good ones at 20-30per cent or more above the initial offering price to allow the preferred accounts to flip the shares and make an immediate profit.

Your major investments should be through a discount brokerage. As mentioned, there are many of them. They all advertise (intermittently) in Barrons , the weekly investment newspaper (which is excellent to keep you up on the news of business and their stock picks are not bad). Since you do not need advice from your broker there is no reason to use a full service brokerage and pay their commissions except for specialized services such as IRAs or educational funds for the kids.

Discount brokers typically give the capability to buy stocks online and pay very low commissions, frequently as low as single digits. I prefer to talk to a human when I buy stock because it is too easy to make a mistake when buying online. That can be very costly and it is always your fault. For instance, staying on the zero key too long. A purchase of 10 shares becomes a purchase of 100 or 1000 or ten thousand shares. The commission costs of buying through a live human are higher than online buying but typically less than 1/3 the cost of buying through a full-service broker. Also, if you want to get out of, or into a stock fast and you cannot reach your broker, which is common with full service brokerage account people at times of market turbulence, you can use the online option. Make sure you understand the commission structure. It is reasonable to check with a number of firms and ask about their costs before picking your discount broker.

Chapter 6:   Getting Advice

You get what you pay for.

Free advice is usually worthless.

Stocks touted in free "newsletters" that you will receive in abundance once you have a brokerage account (---I think all brokerage houses sell your name whether or not they admit it. Probably most of the effective newsletters we will discuss later also sell your name----) are usually paid for by the company being touted. The information is definitely skewed and sometimes outright fabrication.   For about 20 years I was on the board of directors of a small public company—$20-30 million in sales per year—and we were repeatedly solicited to have a letter sent out to tout our stock. We did it once. The letter was beautiful and made our stock sound like the best thing since sliced bread, the stock did not advance.

The internet is filled with tips like this with long stories of little substance urging you to get in "on the ground floor". Please do not fall for this type of advice. It is easy to get into these stocks but virtually impossible to get out without suffering large losses.

The newsletters that are the most valuable and the ones which have made many of us well-off are independent, free of paid advertisements, not affiliated with any brokerage firm or financial institution, and are usually written by one individual, or group under the aegis of one individual, who essentially signs his work. The best ones have usually been around for at least five years. The competition in the field is tremendous. The advice and stock picks should give the ratio of, out of ten, at least three big winners, only two big losers, and five not necessarily big winners but necessarily not big losers, so your capital is not depleted. If the newsletter does not give these results, it won't survive more than two to four years. If the advice is consistently bad, subscriptions are not renewed. Most of the better newsletters do not advertise much, only occasionally in Barrons and occasionally in Investors Business Daily; rarely in the Wall Street Journal; advertisements are expensive. Typically the starting subscription, or trial subscription, is $50-200/year. After the first year this usually goes up to $150-400 per year. Apparently, the newsletter publishers make little on new subscribers. It is in the renewals where the profit is. A newsletter with a bad track record will not get renewals. The readers are selective, and don't want to waste time and money on poor advice. These letters disappear within a few years.

What I want from a newsletter are the ideas and advice of a good stock picker. A good stock picker usually is an intelligent individual with experience in the financial markets or in investment banking. He has spent time working for a major bank, brokerage firm, mutual fund or hedge fund in the analysis side of the business. He knows how to read an annual report (10-K), is independent-minded and has a feel for the markets. However, what really counts is that the stocks he chooses do well, regardless of how he achieves this, and that is why he remains in business. Most writers are also not reluctant to say "sell". And when they give a sell signal always follow their advice.

Newsletters sponsored by brokerage firms or banks almost never say sell until a company is near-bankrupt (for example, Enron, and Global Crossing) because they do not want to offend any large companies.   This is because 1) they usually get a large part of their income from various fees paid by these firms; and 2) brokerage firms that have advised "sell" have been sued for libel.   Newsletter writers do not have this potential conflict of interest.   Their interest is in suggesting investment actions that benefit their subscribers.   Otherwise their readership will dry up very rapidly.

Most good letters have interesting and insightful discussions of economics, international finance, trends, and politics that can lead to increasing sophistication and education of the reader.   Some spend time writing about their hobbies and topics such as rock-and-roll music, motorcycle riding, travel, and health that is fairly useless, but the financial advice is worth wading through this.   One newsletter writer has his own language which he introduces as a glossary of terms which you receive when you first subscribe.

When stocks are suggested there is usually an excellent discussion of the stock and of its investment sector and why prospects for stock price appreciation are good.   It is worthwhile to read these articles because they are educational and it is nice to know what you are buying---***BUT IT IS NOT NECESSARY*** to spend time on these things. You are buying the newsletter because you ***don't*** want to use your own judgment. You want to use the judgment of the newsletter writer. That is why you are subscribing to the newsletter.

Using your own judgment is frequently not good: The apocryphal story is told of the letter writer in the 1960's who suggested that 2 stocks be considered, a successful cement company that had millions in revenues and a company that made an expensive office copier that had only sold a few of its products. The thoughtful investor, at first glance, would invest in the cement company and forget the office device company. The cement company did well. It appreciated about 10% a year. But the office copier company was National Halide, that became Xerox, and the stock appreciated by a factor of 30-50 times. I would have advised not using your judgment, but would have trusted the advice of the newsletter writer and would have bought a small amount of both stocks. This is the principle behind how I suggest using the newsletters.

What I have done is to buy virtually all of the stocks suggested by the newsletter as Best Buys, or Focus Buys, or

Best Pick.   Different newsletters have different terms to designate what their best opinions are.

The problem here is that this sounds like buying a lot of different stocks that requires a lot of money.

The trick is to apportion only a set amount of money to each stock.   It should be small enough so you can buy ten to fifteen different stocks over a short period of time.   Hence if you have $100,000 to invest you might invest $5-6000 in each stock (which I think is too much).   On the other hand if you have only $10,000 to invest you might invest $700-1000 in each stock.   This is why a discount broker is so important. If you have to pay $90-150 per trade, the usual commission charged by a full service brokerage firm, too much of your capital is going on commissions. Whereas, if you are paying only $20-30 or less per trade, small investments are feasible and can be a successful investment strategy.   I currently use a $3000+/- $300 "chip". When the market was way down and my available discretionary capital was smaller, I used $1200+/- $200 as my minimal investment.   I chose these numbers for my chip because a 15 per cent rise would be a decent profit after commissions, and, if on occasion, the entire investment went to zero (which should not happen, but can happen) it would not be a financial catastrophe.   If you cannot afford at least 15 chips of $800-1200, wait until you can, before you start to invest.

Following this concept of "chips" will automatically lead to diversification. And if you follow the advice of a good newsletter, you will invariably make money.

To add safety to your investing, it is worthwhile to sell your losers as soon as they declare themselves as losers. I use a 30-35% stop loss threshold.   I.e., if a stock decreases by more than 30-35 per cent below the price I bought it for, I sell it. Some investors use a 25 per cent threshold, others a 20 per cent threshold.   Less than 20 per cent will lead to losing out on a stock that should be allowed to occasionally dip down before it has a big upward move.   We will discuss selling at length later.

When starting, it is best to buy the stocks that are the new best picks by the newsletter writer, or only the stocks that are especially highlighted in the current newsletter.   Most newsletters will publish their portfolio that frequently includes 20 or more stocks that had been suggested in the past and are being held, usually with a buy recommendation or a buy-up-to-a-certain-price recommendation.   If you have free money you might want to nibble at these stocks later. I don't suggest doing too much of this since many of the stocks that are good picks will have already made much of their upward move, and the stocks that have not gone up yet may be among the inevitable stocks in every stock pickers portfolio that never go up.

Chapter 7: Picking a newsletter

There are two excellent newsletters that you should stay away from. They are Value line and Zacks. They are superb but they supply too much information and too many stocks and they require you to pick and choose.   Although the top 20% of the universe of stocks that they recommend as the best will on average go up, picking which of these stocks will go up is not what you want to do.   In most cases you will guess wrong and there are too many to allow you to buy all of them.   You want a newsletter that picks stock for you to buy and presents only a few stocks that they feel are the best.

   The letter I have been using for the past ten years and that I continue to like is Louis Navalier's Blue Chip Growth Letter.   His picks have been excellent and most of his stocks are stable companies with good revenues that usually do not go down much and usually appreciate handsomely. He tends to get into stocks only after they have made a bit of a move, but his results are good.

Navalier also has other letters that he tries to sell to his Blue Chip Growth subscribers. They are more expensive, more speculative and include more stocks in their portfolios. I have used the Emerging Growth letter and have found it to be more fun if you enjoy speculating but, for me, it has not been more profitable than his premier letter. He also has a Quantum Growth letter which I have not tried. The cost of the Emerging Growth letter is about 4-5 times the cost of the Blue Chip letter and the Quantum Growth letter is about 7-10 times the cost of the Blue Chip letter. In the past I have tried these high priced letters that are spinoffs of a successful primary letter and I have lost money. (I also worry that the writer may start to not give his best suggestions in the primary letter and the emergence of a secondary letter is a signal to stop using that letter writer. So far this has not been the case with Navalier and his Blue Chip Growth letter remains my favorite. A new investor should stick with the primary letter of all those writers with multiple letters.)

The next letter that is excellent for the new investor is Richard E. Band's Profitable Investing. He is knowledgeable, conservative, and his picks rarely go down. He tends to have many small to moderate successes and occasionally a biggy. He suggests mostly stocks that pay dividends and he is well diversified. He does not have secondary letters. He usually has two to six new ideas every month and he is not reluctant to sell.

There is another letter that I have had great success with and that I usually open as soon as it arrives that is technically not written by one individual, but by an organization (or pseudo- organization.). It is the Oxford Club "Communique" (as soon as you subscribe you become a member of the club). It comes out twice a month, with one large letter per month and a supplement on line about the middle of the month. They frequently have a number of short articles, each by a different writer, usually young analysts or occasionally very seasoned stock pickers with usually one or two of their best suggestions along with a well written, concise, interesting discussion of their reasoning. It is not unreasonable to buy many of their suggestions but the trick is to go to the back of the letter and check which stock they have added to their main portfolio. This is the stock to buy. At least two out of three of these stocks will appreciate handsomely and the third usually does not go down by much. The letter also has a few other portfolios in addition to the Oxford Trading portfolio, an aggressive "Ten Bagger of Tomorrow" portfolio, a "Gone Fishing" portfolio that you can buy and hold and a very conservative "All Star" portfolio, all the stocks of which, in my experience, have done well.

They occasionally tout spinoff letters on the internet that cost 5-10 times the cost of the primary letter. They claim a very successful system that in my experience usually does not work as well as the primary letter. Once you are a subscriber to many of these letters your computer will be bombarded by much information and many offers. As noted previously free information is usually worth what you pay for it and the techniques and strategies sold through these "sucker letters" do not usually work as well as their description (vide infra.)

It is worthwhile however, to go to the letters web site every now and then (almost all letters have them) and log in with the user name and password you received when you subscribed. On the website you often find something new between letters. If they have a weekly update it is useful to read it.

Another pair of writers who have led to much of my success are John Dessauer (Investors World) and Richard Young (Intelligence Report). Dessauer was one of the first letters I used, starting in the late 70's and his advice has been excellent. He is the ultimate optimist; rarely suggests selling and almost always gives a bullish story. He was usually right even if it was nerve-wracking to sit through a long market setback without getting out of losers. They do usually come back, however and over the long term I have done very well following his advice. Unfortunately he retired his newsletter a few years ago though he still publishes a weekly hotline on line that does not usually suggest stocks but is an excellent discussion of current economics.

Richard Young's letter is very conservative, almost to a fault. He is enamored with mutual funds (which I do not like) and the ones he picks usually do well. He usually highlights 8-10 stocks every month (not always new stocks) and his picks tend to do well. With each issue he includes a separate section with graphs and tables and very readable discussions of interesting macro-economic data that are usually very enlightening. Every few months he includes a "monster list" of stocks, all of which have a story and have been well vetted. Most are worthwhile. When he removes a stock from this list it is time to sell it. He also has a "monster list" of mutual funds he follows and includes the top 10 stocks held by each fund. It is valuable to compare these lists with your holdings. If you have many of these stocks it means you are in good company. It is also interesting to see the remarkable overlap in the stocks held by the different mutual funds.

Young is a fairly mature stock picker and he tends to not offer many new stocks to buy. Rather he encourages you to hold and to buy more of the stocks he has been suggesting over the past 10 years. Young's stocks have been growing for years and continue to grow.

This week (Sept, 2017) I just received a notice that Young is retiring from letter writing and will spend his time managing the funds of investors who have entrusted him with $500,000 or more. The newsletter will continue but with a new editor. He will probably keep the same format as described above. I hope he will be as good as Young. Time will tell.

One of my favorite letters for new ideas has been Stephen Leeb's letter. A few years ago he left a letter he had edited for years and it immediately deteriorated. I was pleased to find that he started a new letter (The Complete Investor). He presents excellent ideas and over the years his stocks have done well.   He presents a number of portfolios: a Growth Portfolio, which is especially good, an Income Portfolio which is good and a Mutual Fund Portfolio which I personally ignore. He also gives suggestions for aggressive and speculative investors (Fast Track Portfolio) that are interesting but in my experience, tend to be less successful than his usual suggestions in the other portfolios, but are worth gambling on with money you can afford to lose. A new investor should stay away from them.   In addition he presents a list of stocks he has culled from the published holdings of many mutual funds. These stocks are fairly novel but their investment results are mixed.

Over the past 6 years I have begun reading a few letters that have so far done very well. The one I like the best is the Mark Skousen letter (Forecasts and Strategies.) He presents great ideas and is heavy in income producing stocks including closed end investment trusts, master limited partnerships (MLPs), business development companies, and mezzanine finance stocks. Closed end funds and trusts are groups of stocks that trade as a fixed group on the exchanges that were established at some point in the past and that you buy from someone else as compared to the usual mutual funds that you buy directly from the mutual fund. Closed end funds trade at what the market thinks they are worth, which may be greater or less than the net asset value. The net asset value is the market value of the portion of the shares held by the fund that is represented by each share of the fund. The usual mutual fund shares always trade at their net asset value that is calculated every night after close of the major stock exchanges. Mutual funds rarely hold much cash so if a lot of people buy a mutual funds shares the fund has a large infusion of new capital which it must invest, frequently in inopportune markets. If a large number of mutual fund share-holders cash out of a usual mutual fund (they can only sell their shares to the mutual fund itself) the mutual fund must sell enough of the shares they hold in various companies to generate cash to cover the withdrawal.   This can cause the mutual fund to sell at inopportune times.   Since any short or long term capital gains from the sale of shares in companies held by the mutual fund must be passed through to each mutual fund share holder the paradox of having to pay capital gains tax when the value of your holdings has gone down occurs and is most distressing.   This happens if you buy into a mutual fund and pay a high price after many of the stocks it holds have gone up above their initial buy price but these shares are then sold below their price when you got in, but above their initial buy price.   (Also see mutual fund chapter.) Closed end funds do not receive your money when you buy them or give you money when you sell them and hence are not forced to buy or sell shares in the companies they hold, at inopportune times.   Also they do not pass through any capital gains or losses for you to be taxed on.   So these problems do not occur.

 Skousen is also an excellent picker of common stocks and most of his suggestions do well.   In addition he is very good about telling you when to sell, advice you should always follow.

Porter Stansberry's primary letter (Investment Advisor) is very useful. He is fairly conservative and usually gives only one or two suggestions in each newsletter. So far his advice has been fairly good but I am still evaluating him.

Stansberry has a number of spinoffs and other letters published by his company. David Eifrigs letter, Income Intelligence, has been excellent and all of his suggestions give dividends. He also includes a list of "World Dominating Dividend Growers", stocks that have consistently raised their dividends every year. If the dividends are reinvested, the miracle of compound interest will lead to large gains over the years. This group of stocks will be especially valuable for those with retirement 5-10 years in their future.

His other spinoffs have had mediocre results. Extreme Value was a disappointment. Steve Sjuggerud's Truewealth is also published by Stansberry. His results have been OK. Some years ago his indicators put him into a sell mode and he suggested alternate investments. His Icelandic bonds did not do exceptionally well and his collectible coins at best have been mixed. (Collectible coins scare me. The price of a rare coin is completely dependent on its condition or its "grading". The price of a St. Gaudens gold coin graded MS63 was recently $1,195 whereas one graded MS 65 was $1,735. I worry that since the grading is done by an expert (the selling or buying firm) a coin that is MS 65 when you buy it may be graded MS63 when you sell it and you have little recourse re the evaluation.)

One of the negatives associated with any of the Stansberry letters you subscribe to is that you are bombarded with " sucker letters". A sucker letter is an unsolicited letter that suggests that the author has found a hidden opportunity that will result in your getting wealthy in a very short period of time.   The writer will describe the stock or investment vehicle or investment technique in such a way that you cannot figure out what they are selling or which stock they are discussing unless you get this very exclusive report (and the name of the stock) which you will get free when you subscribe to their newsletter at a special introductory (very high) price. They then go on to describe other super winners, usually 3 or 4 events with which they have been successful in the past—not mentioning their losers.   These sucker letters are very skillfully written—apparently you can earn large fees if you know how to write one--- and we all fall for them.   Just remember if it were that easy to hit it big the newsletter writer with the big secret would be keeping it for himself and getting very rich himself, or would be making big bucks running a hedge fund.

New investors should be protected from these sucker traps by the primary newsletter writer.   Stansberry does not do this.

There are three letters that I have found to be useful that are less personality letters and more theory letters; that is, they follow certain basic ideas and suggest stocks that fit with their principles. The theory letter that I have the most experience with is the Dow Theory Forecasts letter. They follow a large number of quality stocks, most of which are solid blue chip stocks and using the theories worked out by Dow in the late nineteenth, early twentieth century they present a Focus Buy List, a Buy List and a Long Term Buy List.   They highlight at least one stock (not necessarily new) in each letter and constantly re-discuss stocks on the various lists. Their stock suggestions are excellent, though rarely very exciting. You usually will not go wrong if you stick first with their Focus List, then their Buy List and then their Long Term Buy List.   Their evaluation of sectors of the market and the market itself using the Dow theory to suggest whether the market is bullish or bearish are quite interesting.   The Dow theory is occasionally a self-fulfilling prophecy, since so many professionals follow it.   They periodically present a list of monitored stocks with current opinions.   Not all of these stocks are on their buy lists and it is useful to check on their opinion re stocks you already own or that are being suggested by other newsletters.

Dow Theory Forecasts has a spinoff that I have used with mixed results called Upside. The stocks touted here tend to be smaller cap stocks than in the premier newsletter and are significantly more speculative. They also present a large number of ideas and for the new investor with a small amount of capital it can be overwhelming. I have given up on the letter. Stick with the premier letter and mainly their focus list when getting started.

The next theory letter that I use is the Cabot letter. Their main letter, which I use less now, presents two portfolios. One is set up according to the principles of Benjamin Graham who developed the method of value investing in the 30's. (His book,"The Intelligent Investor" is still worth reading to understand the usual method for evaluating stocks that is used almost universally.) At that time data on companies and their balance sheets were not as available as they are now and he knew how to evaluate a balance sheet. Value investors—evaluating assets, revenues, sales, expenses, debt, cost to reproduce the company, cash on hand, free cash flow, market niche, etcetera--- over the long run are usually successful. (Warren buffet is a value investor; apparently he studied under Graham.) Over the short run, however they might not do so well. To be a value investor you must have patience.

In addition to the portfolio that follows the Graham principles there is also a "wise owl" portfolio that also performs fairly well.

The Cabot letter that I currently use is the Cabot Undervalued Stock Advisor edited by Crista Huff. She puts out a weekly review of her stocks on the internet. The problem is she follows a large number of stocks. However the few she terms "strong buy" usually do the best. Her growth portfolio also tends to do well.

The third theory letter that is fairly good is the Morningstar letter (Stock Investor). They are conservative and most of their picks do well. The have a "Tortoise" and a "Hare" portfolio. The latter is more speculative but not by much. They (as do some other letters) give a buy- up- to price and this can occasionally lead to frustration because the buy- up- to price is less than the price the stock is trading at, so theoretically you should not buy it. It is best to do as they say. Often the price will come down over the next few days or weeks. They also suggest a "minimal" sell price which is useful to help determine when to take profits. The Morningstar Letter and the Dow theory Forecasts letter also includes a large list of stocks with their current rating so stocks that you are holding or that have been suggested by other newsletters can be checked.

A spinoff of the Morningstar Stock Investor I have been using recently is the Morningstar Dividend Investor.   The suggestions for dividend paying stocks are conservative and excellent.   I have only been getting it on and off for a few years; so far the advice has been good.

Another good general letter which I have not used but one of my friends has been subscribing to for years is the Motley Fool Stock Advisor.   They are now predominantly on line and do not send a hard copy newsletter by mail. I have been looking at it recently and the ideas of the two editors are interesting and some of them have done very well.

There are a number of other useful letters: Bryan Perry's " Cash Machine", Thom Huchinson's " High Income Factor", Nathan Slaughter's "High Yield Investing", Zach Scheidt's "Lifetime Income Report", for income stocks.
Louis Basenese's "True Alpha", Teeka Tiwaris' "Palm Beach Letter", Michael Robinsons "Nova –X Report", Keith Fitz-Gerald's "Money Map Report", Ray Blanco's "Technology Profits Confidential",   Bill Spetrino's "Dividend Machine", for novel ideas.

We have reviewed a number of investment newsletters.   The opinions I have expressed are my own and just opinions and may be wrong.   I am only expressing how the individual letters have worked for me, following the advice as I interpret it and describing my individual experience.   Others may have more favorable or less favorable experiences with these letters.   But this is a starting point.

In summary:

1) Buy a good newsletter and follow the advice you are buying; they all have websites and can be found easily on the internet. For the new investor the best are Navalier, Band, or Skousen and one of the general letters: Leeb, Dow Theory Forecasts, or Morningstar.

2) Invest small amounts in virtually all the stocks suggested especially those that are highlighted or strongly recommended. Do not pick and choose. They are all at best only 65% right.

3) Develop discipline to sell when a stock has dropped a set percentage (>35%,>30%,>25%--- not if it only drops 20%)

4) When the newsletter you are using says sell---sell, don't wait.

5) Avoid spinoffs of the great letters.

6) Recognize and avoid sucker letters.

See the addendum chapters on what to do during the current economic environment.

Chapter 8: Options: Avoid or Be Very Careful

When you subscribe to any financial newsletter, as noted before, you will be bombarded with letters to buy something else, another service or letter that will immediately make you very wealthy.   Virtually all of these communications are wildly exaggerated, but none so much as the ones that tout the use of options. Don't fall for it.

Briefly, options are contracts that you buy that give you the right to buy (call options) or sell (put options) 100 shares of a stock at a set price for a set period of time (until the expiration date of the option).   Thus, if you think stock in QRS Company that is selling for $20 is going to go up to $25 within one to six months you can buy an option to purchase 100 shares of QRS for $20 (strike price) at any time in the next 3 months that will cost you e.g., $2.50 per share. Hence, for $250 you are buying the right to buy 100 shares at $20 and will get the upside potential of the stock without shelling out $2000 to buy 100 shares of the stock now and without risking any more money than that which you paid for the option (plus transaction costs). If the stock drops below the strike price, $20 in this case, the option will expire worthless. If the stock goes up to $25 before expiration of the option you can either exercise the option (buy the shares for $20/share) and immediately sell the shares for $25 and net $2500 minus $2000 (the cost of 100 shares) minus $250 (the cost of the option) minus transaction costs ($20-100), i.e. you will net about $200 which is a $200/250 or 80% profit. Or you can sell the option near expiration for $500 which is what it is worth if the stock is selling for $25 plus a small premium without exercising.

Alternatively, if you think QRS is going to go down you can buy a put option which gives you the right to sell 100 shares of

QRS at $20/share for three months, regardless of the market price. If QRS goes from $20/share to $15/ share during these three months you can exercise your option, i.e. buy 100 shares of QRS on the market for $1500 and sell it to the guy you bought the put option from, for $2000 making $500 profit (minus the $250 you paid for the option minus transaction costs –or about $200 again) without selling short or taking any risk of losing more than the cost of the option. SOUNDS GREAT!!   making lots of money (80% profit) in a short period of time.   The problem is that most options are sold at a loss or expire worthless, and most option buyers consistently lose money.

This occurs for two reasons:

First, options are time dependent and the premium (cost of the option above what it would be worth if it were exercised on the day it was purchased) is set by the options market-maker who figures out what the chances are that the stock price will go up within the time period, figures out how optimistic the public is and then sets the price accordingly.   Moreover, the option seller who theoretically already owns the 100 shares, will only sell an option at a price he is willing to sell the shares for. So the specialist and the option seller, both usually more sophisticated than the option buyer, sets the price so that rarely, and only if there is a surprise large move in the price of the stock, will the option buyer make any money. Consider, to make money in the described QRS call trade, the stock will have to trade by the end of the contract period for greater than about $23 or up 15% . This rarely occurs unless the stock is very volatile—and in that case the $20 call will cost much more, e.g. $3.50 or $4.00 per share.

- So THERE ARE NO BARGAINS IN PUTS AND CALLS.

Secondly, with purchase of stocks, if you buy 100 shares of QRS for $2000 you can sit on it for years, if it does not go up much over the short term. That is not the case with options.   They are wasting assets. Even if the stock does not go down, or if it goes up only a little bit, the option decreases in value almost daily. A call option for QRS stock bought on Mar 12 for 2.50 that will expire on May 20 (they expire on the third Friday of each month) will be worth about 1.60 on April 1 and about 70 cents on May 1 and about .10 on May 15 if the stock remains at 20.   Frequently the value of an option may increase soon after you buy it, but usually the spike is transient and you miss it or you will reason:

"Aha—I was right, I will stick with my decision and make much money because of the leverage"--- and invariably the option price will fall and you will lose it all.

Stay away from buying options.

(Note: one option letter I (foolishly) subscribed to claimed profits on virtually all of its suggested trades.

#1—it was impossible to get the option they suggested at the price they suggested because the price was quoted as higher when you wanted to buy it.

#2----they did not tell you when to sell and considered that the option was profitable if it ever went above your buy price. E.g., if the QRS call rose from 2.50 to 2.75 the day after you bought the call, that was a 10% profit in that trade (although you would never sell it after one day if it was going up) even if, for the subsequent life of the call option, the price never went above $1.75 again.)

I have never successfully traded options. If you want to try, you must watch the market constantly and be very nimble, sitting in front of the computer seven hours/day ready to take profits or cut losses immediately.   Options are either very volatile or they just uniformly, inexorably, go down.

Although not for the new or small investor there is a way to usually make money with options. It is essentially playing as if you are the "house" or casino owner.

That is, to sell covered calls:

For example, you buy 200 shares of QRS for $4000 ($20 per share), you sell two call option contracts for $2.50 to allow the buyer to buy the shares at $20 for 3 months. You get $500 minus transaction costs. At the end of the contract, in 3 months, if the stock is at $20 or above it is called away; i.e., it is sold to the call option owner. You get $4000 minus transaction costs.

Basically you have put up about $3550 and you receive about $3950 for a $400 profit or about 11% in 3 months. Not bad—however if the stock falls below 17.50 you lose money. If it appreciates above 22.50 you participate in none of the upside. That's not fun and potentially (though not usually) a losing strategy .

(Rarely opportunities to make out well, because of irrational markets, do come along. Recently, on recommendation of one of my usually conservative letters, I bought 100 shares of a company for $5000 ($50/share) and sold a $55 three month call for $4.00. This call was very much "out of the money" and the premium I got was extraordinarily large. If it is called away I will make about 18% on my investment, $5500 on $4600, minus transaction costs. If it falls below 46 I am a loser. These opportunities are rare.)

There are two other strategies for making money that are touted by sucker letters that can be lucrative but are potentially dangerous. The first involves selling puts. These puts obligate the seller to buy 100 shares of a company for a price much lower than the current price. For example: you sell a put for 100 shares of XYZ stock for $15 when the stock is currently selling for $20 and you get 50 cents/share or $50, the premium, immediately. This obligates you to buy the stock for $15/share for the life of the put, e.g. 90 days. The chances that the stock will drop to $15 or less is very unlikely and chances are you will keep the premium as the option expires worthless. Usually the premiums are relatively low if the price is safely lower than the current price. This means that the seller often sells many contracts; e.g., here ten puts to make $500. If there is a sudden unexpected drop in the stock price to below $15 the put seller will have to come up with a large amount of money. This can be a catastrophe. It happens rarely but when it does occur it can destroy an investor.

The other strategy is less dangerous but is not necessarily the best use of your money; and you can lose a lot. You buy a long term call in the money on an expensive stock that you would not mind owning for a period of time. Apple is selling for 162 today, September 2017. You can buy a $135 call for April 2018 for $30. The more the call is in the money the less the premium, $3 in this case. You then sell a $170 call for December for $5.50. If the stock goes over $170 the call will be exercised. You then exercise

your call i.e. you will get 100 shares for $13,500.   You give the
100 shares to the holder of the $170 call and get $17,000.   You get
a profit of $3500 plus $550 you got when you sold the $170 call
minus $3000 you paid for the $135 call, for a net profit of $1050
(minus transaction costs).   Not bad, about >30% on the $3000
you put out, after about 3 months.   However, if the stock does not
go to >$170 and your stock is not called, if the stock goes to about
<$156 you lose money, because the price you paid for the long
term option, $3000, begins to deteriorate.   You can probably sell it
for about $2400 for a loss of $600 or greater.   If you work out the
numbers you will probably break even if the stock stays above
$158.

Summary: A new investor (and most other investors) should stay
away from options.

Chapter 9: When To Sell

First: Always sell when the newsletter that suggested the stock, says to sell it.

 Second: Set a mental stop-loss number and try to stick with it. I use 30-35%. If a stock falls by 30-35% below the price I paid for it, I sell it. It is hard to sell because it makes us face the fact that we were *WRONG*. When we sell, it means we have given up hope, which is difficult to do. But if we are to play the market we must accept that we (and all of our advisors) will be wrong at least one-third of the time. If we cut our losses, before they become excessive, the winners should, by far, over balance the losers.

The stop loss should be mental. That is, do not formally tell your broker to sell if a stock goes below a set price (which you can do). Occasionally, if there are a lot of stop-loss orders in a specialists book he will dip the price to take out the stop-loss orders and generate stock to be sold to someone else. Keep an eye on your stocks and put in orders to sell when your mental stop has been reached. Use the price at the end of the day; do not use the intra- day price. The stock may go up immediately after you sell it – this is called being "whipsawed". Don't mourn when this happens; it is part of the game. Most often, after you have sold a stock that has already gone down by 30-35% it will continue to go down.

Some investors use "trailing" stops. Basically, instead of using the buy-in price from which to calculate your 30%-off sell price, you adjust the base price to be the highest price the stock has achieved since you bought it. Thus if you are using a 30% drop as your sell-threshold; i.e., if you bought a stock for $20 you would sell it if it dipped below $14. If it went up to $30 you would subsequently sell it if it dropped below $21 (30% of $30 is $9; $30 minus $9 equals $21). This becomes unwieldy if followed rigidly but the use of mental stops allows you to be flexible. For instance, if I have been sitting on a stock that has gone nowhere in 6 months I might consider a 20-25% stop. If a stock is very volatile and I am impressed with it, I may allow it to go down by up to 45-50% (rarely). On the other hand if a stock has gone up by 60% and then something changes and it starts slipping I might get out after it dips by 15% off its high.

Taking profits is the hardest decision to make. As a rule of thumb, stocks that go up usually continue to go up and riding your winners is usually a good thing to do, so I rarely sell winners.

However, it is reasonable to sell some of the shares after a stock has had a good move.   In those instances, first, if a stock has gone up by over 100% take out the initial investment and let the rest ride. Another reasonable technique, in stocks that have appreciated but not over 100%, take the profit off the table and leave the amount that is your usual chip in the stock.   Do not hesitate to sit on odd lots—if you own 100 shares that have gone up 60%, there is no reason you cannot sell 40 shares and keep 60 shares.

Also, although it is difficult to do, keep an eye out for "flare" stocks.   These are stocks that go up exceedingly rapidly because of a novelty product or an extraordinary event.   These stocks can "fizzle" just as rapidly. A recent case in point is Crocs—they manufacture very colorful plastic shoes for children.   The stock rapidly went up to 5-6 times its IPO price. A runup based on the whims of kids is dangerous and the stock dropped below its initial offering price in a few weeks.   The best thing is to take some money off the table, i.e., sell some of the stock when it appreciates by 75% in less than 2 months.   (As of May 2008 I was concerned about Apple which flared because of the ipod but continued to go up, and certain fertilizer stocks which have flared because of a perceived grain shortage but then went down rapidly.)

And of course, always remember, you are investing to be able to afford to live a better life. If you are buying a house, need money for your daughter's college tuition or want a special vacation or an impressive gift for your wife, do not hesitate to cash in some of your winners. Your wealth is only numbers on a ledger sheet until you use it.

Note on Buying and Selling:

Do not put in market orders. The market can change rapidly. Find out the bid and ask prices; that is, the price someone who wants to buy the stock is willing to pay for it and the price someone who owns the stock is willing to sell it for. If you want to buy, put in a bid slightly higher than the asking price. If you want to sell, offer the stock at a price slightly lower than the bid price. You will usually get it at the market price anyway. Using a market order is OK only if the stock is traded on the NYSE, never on NASDAQ, pink sheets or foreign exchanges. Your purchase may not go through but this is better than putting in a market order to purchase a stock with a bid and ask of $35-35.50 and paying $41 for it.

Setting a price for buying or selling is called a limit order. For example, QRS stocks last sale was $20. The current bid price (price someone has offered to buy a share for) is $19.50; the ask price (the price someone is willing to sell a share for) is

$20.50. If I definitely want to buy the shares I will put in an offer

to "buy the stock at $20.75 or better" (just over the asking price)

and will probably get it for $20.55. If I really wanted to sell the

stock I would put in an order to "sell at $19.25 or better" (slightly

below the bid price) and would probably sell it for $19.45. If you

are not too eager to buy (or sell) you might put your desired price

somewhere between the bid and the ask price. Your order may or

may not be filled. Market orders always get filled but your price

may be very far from the bid/ask values and are almost at the

complete discretion of the market maker, also called a specialist,

the individual or firm that acts as the middle man buying the shares

from the seller and selling the shares to the buyer. Limit orders

are especially important in stocks that have a small number of

shares that trade each day (a small float) such as small

capitalization companies (small caps = total value of company=

stock price X number of shares outstanding. If less than 2 billion

dollars they are called small caps.) and foreign companies. When

buying stocks on the NY stock exchange, limit orders are less

important, but I always use them.

Tax-Time Selling

If you have gains from sales of appreciated stocks, which you invariably will have, the autumn is the time to exercise discipline and take losses to offset the profits and decrease your capital gains tax.   Occasionally a stock will go down without your noticing it and may drift below 30-40% of what you paid for it (which should not happen because you have mental stops at 25-35% of your buy-in price and you should have sold it; but for some reason you wanted to hold it) or a stock has gone down but not yet to its mental stop price and you want to hold it.   This assumes that the newsletter that originally suggested it, is still suggesting that you buy it or hold it.   It is wise to use the changes that usually occur in autumn, to take your losses.

Usually the nadir of the market occurs in early October, and then there is a rally into mid-January.   This occurs for a variety of reasons. It is usually attributed to mutual funds or large institutions (such as pension funds) selling their losers in late September and early October and buying popular stocks that have been winners, in late October, November and December. They do this so the losers will not appear on the end-of-year statements. And the winners will appear there.   This makes the mutual fund shareholders think the fund manager is brilliant and they throw more money at him.   Also, late September and early October are relatively dead times re company reports about sales and profits. The reports of the second quarter results are usually all in by early September and reports of the third quarter results (July, August, September,) don't appear until late October or November., so there is no news to stimulate buying.   Also stocks usually go up during late November into December ("Santa Claus rally") and into January and February because, in addition to cosmetically making a mutual funds results look better, there is new money from retirement accounts that come into the market and into the funds managed by institutions.   (This seasonality occurs in about 3 out of 4 years—it did not happen in 2000 when the supreme court elected W and it was muted in 2007 with the housing mortgage debacle.)   In any case, we can use this seasonality to take losses, and sometimes benefit as we take the losses.

There is a rule that you cannot take a loss on a stock if you buy it back in less than 30 days.   To maximize the possible benefits of tax loss selling and seasonality I will buy another chips worth of a losing stock on about October 10-25.   For example, if I bought 150 shares of QRS stock for $20 ($3000) and it goes down to $8 (I wasn't paying attention) I will buy another 375 shares for $3000, my "chip". I will hold the shares for over 30 days and then

I will sell the original 150 shares on December 28—it must be sold before December 31 to count for a loss in that tax year. By then the stock may have appreciated, e.g. to $9.50 I will sell the original 150 shares and credit a loss of $1675 plus transaction costs, i.e. $3000 original cost minus $1375 I got by selling the 150 shares (minus costs). However I have actually cut my loss by the 1.50 appreciation of the 375 shares or $582.50 and I will hold the 375 shares to get further possible appreciation during the first quarter of the new year, when stocks usually go up.

By using this technique you should not have to pay much in capital gains taxes and you will still retain an interest (and larger number of shares) in stocks that might appreciate. Sometimes you are throwing good money after bad but in my experience on balance it works out to my benefit. Seasonalities are statistical and do not always occur. Thus "sell in May and go away until after Labor Day" does not always work. Remember, timing the market is dangerous because most gains for the year in the market occur during only 10-25 days during a year and if you are out of the market on those days you may lose out on all the gains for the year.

Chapter 10:   More On Why I Avoid Mutual Funds; The Use of Closed End Funds, ETF's and Index Funds

Theoretically, mutual funds are set up by a group of people pooling their money, electing a board of directors who answer to the people who put up the money.   The board finds a manager who is very smart, they bargain a fair (low) price for him to manage the fund and change managers (fire him) if his investment results are not good.   If the results of the fund are consistently bad, those who put up the money vote out the board of directors, and elect a different board that will manage the money more successfully.

Sounds good but that is not how it really works.

Usually a mutual fund is started by a firm that will do the managing. The firm sets up a hand-picked board of directors. The firm may then advertise to say how great their firm, or potential manager, is and solicit money from investors to set up the fund. Usually, however, the firm goes to brokerage houses or to customers men who deal with small investors and entices them to push shares in their mutual fund to their customers by offering them high commissions, larger than 5%. Hence if the investor puts up $1000 for 100 shares in the mutual fund, $50 or more will go to the broker and $950 or less will be invested (part of frontloading).

When many of the shares are sold, the originating firm will then invest the money and charge, typically, a management fee of 2 %-- or more of the total assets per year. The manager will, hopefully, pick the right stocks and the value of each share of the portfolio will go up and the shares will rapidly generate a 5 per cent profit to make up for the front load and greater than 2 percent profit to make up for the management fee and everyone will be happy. However, if the stock picks are not so good, the value of the fund shares will go down by the front load amount and by the yearly management fee. The managing group gets their 2 per cent, or more, regardless of whether the value of the shares in the mutual fund goes up or down. The mutual fund shareholders get to vote on usually 1/3 of the directors each year and theoretically can eventually throw out the directors of a poorly performing fund, but this rarely happens, primarily because most shareholders don't vote, and secondly because only one slate of director candidates is offered with no alternatives.   The only option the small investor really has is to cash in his shares, usually with a big loss. Moreover, as noted in Chapter 7, a mutual fund investor may end up paying capital gains taxes even though his mutual fund shares have lost money.   Read the mutual fund prospectus, which most people don't read, but must be supplied, by law, when you buy into a mutual fund. It is all there in black and white.

I would stay away from mutual funds.

However, the concept that a small investor can benefit from pooling his money with other small investors and using a stock guru is not really such a bad idea, and it is possible to get these benefits without many of these liabilities, using a closed end fund. . Closed end funds do not have front-end costs and trade on the exchanges as if they were common stocks. The commission you pay is the same as if you purchased shares of stock in one company.   Moreover, these funds frequently trade at a discount to net asset value. This means that a share in the closed end fund that you buy for $9 may represent $10 worth of stock in various companies. Because you are buying part of an ongoing portfolio of stocks that was capitalized years ago, the fund, from someone who owns the shares, representing part of the portfolio, and not from the fund itself, whether the share price goes up or down and whether more people buy or sell shares in the fund does not determine whether the fund has to sell, or buy stock in other companies, i.e. add to or liquidate stock holdings in the fund . Puchases of stock do not have to occur at inopportune times and stock holdings do not have to be sold to generate cash to buy out fund shareholders who want to get rid of their shares. Capital gains occur only when it is appropriate to take them. Moreover, closed end funds usually do not have high management fees. The cost of these fees is readily available, and if greater than 1.5 per cent, I suggest buying a different closed end fund. Occasionally, funds with high management fees trade with a higher discount-to-net-asset value.

ETFs (Exchange Traded Funds) are similar to conventional mutual funds except that the stocks held in an ETF are not changed very often and are relatively disciplined. The originator of the ETF must buy stock only in the designated country or sector of the market and which stocks it holds are not subject to change very

often.   Hence there is no guru who decides what to buy or sell- so
no high salaries are generated and maintenance expenses are
modest. In addition the shares trade at any time of the day on the
exchanges as if they were a stock and the net asset value (the price)
is calculated by the minute not by the end of the day.   There is
also no frontloaded commission and you are purchasing the shares
from another stock holder, not necessarily from originator of the
ETF.   If you want to use mutual type funds, go with ETF's or
closed end funds.   They are very liquid, have a narrow bid and ask
price and are easily and rapidly bought and sold through your
regular discount stock broker.   Beware, your broker will denigrate
these funds and will try to steer you to conventional mutual funds--
-his commission is significantly higher with conventional mutual
funds, especially new ones.

Index funds are ETFs that are baskets of stocks that include
all stocks in a specific index, such as the Dow Jones Average, or
the S&P 500 or NASDAQ 100.   These funds, obligatorily must
contain every stock in the index they are following in the
proportion they exist in the index.   Only if the index changes the
stocks it contains, does the manager have to do anything, and then
he does not get the opportunity to make any decision.   The yearly
management fee for an index fund should be, and usually is, about
½ per cent or less and always below 1 per cent.

ETFs and closed end funds now come in many varieties. Each is a basket of stocks, either reflecting an index or representing a portfolio of stocks in a specific sector. Thus, if you think that Germany, India, Switzerland, China or Eastern Europe is going to do well, you can buy an ETF or closed end fund, paying only a usual stock commission, that has invested in many different stocks in that country. Similarly, there are ETFs that are portfolios of biotech stocks, banking stocks, homebuilder stocks or technology stocks, that are very liquid and can be easily bought and sold whenever the market is open.

Who should invest in these ETFs and/or closed end funds?

1) If your funds are limited and you think the market will go up, buy a general index ETF, e.g. the Dow Jones Average, such as a Spyder, or the S&P 100. The costs are low and you will benefit, or get hurt, with any moves in the general market. Interestingly, most mutual funds, with high front-loads, and high management fees, do not do as well as the index funds. My techniques, using newsletters, usually do better than the indexes.

2) If you feel that a sector or a country, such as big pharmaceutical firms, or Taiwan, is going to do well, and you want to have an interest in that industrial sector or in that country, it is appropriate to buy ETFs or closed end funds that invest in those areas.

3) A number of the newsletters I use, and that I suggest that you use, are recommending ETFs, and closed end funds more often.   Take their advice; the newsletters are usually right.

As I am writing this edition in the summer of 2017   ETFs are becoming more and more popular because of the low management fees and the disciplined make-up of the fund according to which niche you want to invest in.   Some of the ETFs have grown to own a large percentage of the stocks in a particular niche.   This raises the dangerous possibility that a sudden run on the ETF could result in the overabundance of indiscriminant sales of all stocks in that niche and may result in a marked drop in the prices of all stocks in that particular niche.   This has not happened yet but has made some investors wary of the safety of very specialized ETFs.

Chapter 11:   How to Follow Your Stocks

1) Thank God for the internet!!

Every brokerage house has a website, and you can get onto the website and see your account at any hour of the day or night, and assess the value of any stock that you hold. If the broker you use does not offer this feature, change brokers.

2) Check your account at least 3 times per week—every day is OK but do not become obsessed with it and more than once per day is not necessary.

3) You are checking your account for 3 reasons:

A: To make sure your orders were carried out successfully, and to determine if trades went off and at what price.   Remember, we are only using limit orders, not market orders, so occasionally a stock we wanted to buy suddenly went up beyond our buy price, and we did not buy it, or a stock we wanted to sell dropped below our asking price and was not sold.   It is important to know this because we may raise our buying price or lower our asking price. Also, occasionally errors occur, our fault or the fault of the broker. If caught early, these mistakes can usually be fixed without any loss, or without much loss.   If not fixed soon, they can become a problem.

B. To check to see that individual stocks have not fallen much below your mental stop value—so you can sell it and cut your losses.

C. To check how you are doing.   This is done by going to the bottom line.   The total performance of your portfolio is what counts, not the performance of individual stocks and that is what you should watch.   Some brokerage houses may give the total value as of the night before, even at 11:30 PM on Thursday the total amount given will be that of the close at 4:00 PM on Wednesday.   To get to the current account value for that day, go to "positions" and scroll down to the bottom line.   The movement of the total value of the account will usually be in the same direction as the S&P 500, and hopefully it should go up by at least the same percentage, or better, and should not go down by more than the S&P.

Chapter 12: Margin Accounts and Futures

When you buy stocks you have to pay for them.

You can pay all in cash, or money transfer from a bank, or you can borrow some of the money from the brokerage firm.   The broker holds the stock (in "street name") and when you sell the stock, you pay back what you borrowed.   While the stock sits in your account you pay interest monthly, about 4-5 per cent per year; it varies with the prime rate and the magnitude of the loan.   In order to do this, you must open a "margin" account.   To open a margin account, most firms require that you have at least $25,000 in cash or in stocks and bonds in the account.   The interest rate is so reasonable because it is usually a no-risk loan for the broker. He has the stock as collateral and if the stock goes down, and you do not come up with more cash he will sell the stock, take back what was borrowed and give you what is left.

Typically they will lend you up to about 50 per cent of the purchase price, and will send you a request for more money (a "margin call") when their loan is more than 60% of the current price. If you don't meet the margin call, they will sell you out, pay themselves the amount of the loan and credit you with the rest.

Thus if you buy 150 shares of QRS stock for $20 ($3000) you can pay them $1500 and borrow $1500 from them. If the stock goes to $30/share you can sell it (150 shares for $4500), they take back their $1500 and you get to keep the remaining $3000. Since you have only had to put up $1500 you essentially have doubled your money on a 50% move in the stock ($20 to $30 is a 50% move). This is called leverage.

Sounds great, and is great if the stock goes up, which happens often, but not always. When the stock goes down the leverage continues to occur but in the opposite direction. If the stock goes from $20 to about $16.75. you will get a margin call. If you do not come up with more money, they will sell you out because your equity is only about 40 per cent; at $16.75 your 150 shares of QRS stock is worth about $2500—you owe $1500 so your equity is only worth about 40% of the total value. If they sell you out in a down market they may only get $15 per share for a total of $2250. They will take their $1500 back and you will get the rest, $750. Thus on a 25 per cent move downward, from $20 to $15. you will have sustained a 50 per cent loss (from the $1500 you put up to the $750-minus transaction costs, which you received after you did not meet the margin call.) That's also called leverage.

So why have a margin account?

First, for convenience. If you buy a stock, you don't have to come up with the money right away. In a cash account you have to have the money in the account already or get it into the account within one to two days. It used to be five days; it isn't anymore. They sell you out regardless of how much equity you have in the account. Second, 15-25% margin is usually not dangerous and the leverage can increase your percent gain (and unfortunately your percentage loss). The key is to never allow the margin, (i.e., loan, to exceed 30 per cent of the equity in your account so you have a large safety moat before you get a margin call, which happens whenever margin goes to about 60%. To keep the margin under 30 per cent, you don't necessarily have to put up more money.

You can generate money to keep the margin amount low, or to satisfy a margin call, by selling stocks in your account. You do not necessarily have to sell the stock you took the loan on. When margin gets large, or there is a margin call, that is the time to recheck if any of your stocks are close to your mental stop, or have gone up so high that you feel it is time to take some profits.

The message concerning margin is:

1) Use margin for convenience; do not fear a margin account.

2) Never let the margin amount get out of control, always keep it less than 30 per cent.

3) To keep margin under control, first sell your losers, then take some profits.

4) Do not use margin in your conservative account, your retirement account (it is illegal) or in your income account, i.e. the account in your spouse's name.

Futures

Unless you have money to burn, and very deep pockets, stay away from futures contracts. They are very dangerous because they are the only investment vehicle where you can lose more money than you put up to consummate the transaction; i.e. in most investments you can only lose the money you put up to enter the investment; your equity can go to zero. With futures contracts you can be sold out and must come up with more money in addition to your initial investment which has gone to zero.

How can this happen? It is basically because the price of commodities, currencies, or financial instruments, such as treasury bills, usually do not move much, and hence the leverage allowed with these contracts is enormous. As demonstrated above, leverage can move both ways.

To illustrate we will discuss silver:

As of August 29, 2017 the contract for December silver was trading at $17.64. A silver contract is for 5000 ounces of silver, so the owner of this futures contract will be paid $88,200 for the contract, on the third Friday of December 2017. If the owner of the contract bought the contract for $16.00 per ounce, he paid $80,000 for the contract and when he sells, it he will make $8,200 profit on the contract. If he paid $19.50 /ounce for the contract, he will have paid $97,500 for the contract, and will lose $9,300 when the contract is exercised. So what is the big deal? This is only a loss of about 9.5% or a gain of about 10.25% The big deal is that traditionally commodities do not move very much---the last decade has been extraordinary for commodity price movements-- and traditionally, the buyer of a futures contract only has to put up 5-10 per cent of the total value of the contract. The rest is margin—for which there is no interest because the contract is a commitment to buy (or sell) something in the future and no actual money changes hands. It is the commitment that changes in value. Thus, by putting up about $5000 to $8000 the buyer controls and has the responsibility to fulfill a contract worth over $90,000. Since there are 5000 ounces, each dollar change in the price of an ounce of silver changes the value of the contract by $5000, or each change of one penny, equates to a change of $50. In the usual market the price of silver, about $9.00 per ounce until late 2006, would rarely fluctuate by more than 25 cents ($1250 per contract). In mid 2008, silver was fluctuating from $16.00 up to over $20.00, and back again over a period of weeks. Since the buyer is only putting up the value of a $1.80 to $2.00 move in silver, if the price of an ounce of silver goes down by about $1.00 he must meet a margin call or be sold out. If silver drops to $17.00 per ounce (from $18.29) there will be a margin call. If it is not answered with more money the position will be sold, possibly at $16.00 if the market continues to go down.   The contract holder will be wiped out—zero equity and he is legally bound to pay the additional money he lost.   For example, he lost $18.29 minus $16.00 or $2.29/ounce, which is equal to $11,450 and he only had $9000 in equity, so he must come up with an additional $2,450.   When commodity or currency or financial futures go against you, you can lose a lot of money very fast.

All of the commodities and financial futures contracts, wheat, corn, cattle, oil, gasoline, gold, Japanese yen, Swiss francs, T-bills, etcetera, work the same way with huge leverage and enormous opportunities for gain--- and for loss.

Note- Futures contracts are very important for commodity users, and commodity producers, as they smooth out the fluctuations in the market and make it possible for both users and producers to plan ahead and have a guaranteed price they will pay for, or receive from the sale of a commodity.

Thus hypothetically, Sweettooth Chocolate Company in January of 2017 will buy a contract for ten tons of cocoa beans for about $2800 per ton, to be delivered in December 2017. Sweettooth Company is now guaranteed that they will get the 10 tons of cocoa beans they need to manufacture chocolate in

December and they know how much they will have to pay for it.
The grower of the cocoa beans now knows that he is guaranteed
$2800 per ton of the cocoa beans he produces so he can be sure of
a certain profit. If the price of cocoa beans goes up because there
is a cocoa blight he will still only get what he guaranteed to sell his
cocoa for, and the Sweettooth Company will not have to pay more
than the contracted price. On the other hand, if the price of cocoa
goes down, because the sunshine and the rain are just right and
there is a huge surplus of cocoa beans produced, the seller will still
get his $2800 per ton, and the candy company will still have to pay
the agreed on price, even though the company may be able to get
the cocoa cheaper on the open spot market. Thus, the chocolate
company, and the farmer who hold the contract until expiration
when the farmer delivers the cocoa to the chocolate company who
accepts the cocoa and pays the agreed price, benefit from having a
futures market. It is not quite so simple, but this is the general
idea.

The grease that makes these markets move smoothly are the
speculators who are not producers, or users, of the commodity, but
buy a contract because they think it will go up, or sell short a
contract if they think the value will go down. The speculators
ensure that the producers get a fair price, and that the users are not
taken advantage of.

The small investor usually loses because the conventional way of dealing in commodities is used against him. Conventionally, "the trend is your friend". The futures trader waits until a trend up or down is established, i.e., the contract price has gone up consistently over a few days, and then the small investor hops on. Typically, very soon after a trend develops itself, the price "corrects", goes down to almost the level at which the trend began. This is usually enough of a drop so there is a margin call. (The other conventional rule for trading commodities is to never meet a margin call, because the margin call is a "sign" that the trend is broken and going in the wrong direction.) The small investor is sold out, hopefully with some capital remaining but most often he is completely wiped out. The trend then usually reasserts itself after the correction.

If you have enough play money to commit 30-40per cent of a contracts total value, about $28000 to $38000 for a silver contract, and if you can consistently meet margin calls you may possibly make a small percentage profit by buying futures for the long term. This implies very deep pockets, and unless he is stupid, naïve, suicidal or just plain crazy, the small investors should *NOT* consider trading futures.

Incidentally, the funds that trade commodities usually lose money for the small investor. The fund management charges outrageous management fees, and like a hedge fund, do not suffer losses if their investments are bad, but take 20-50 per cent of any profit that is generated. If you have a strong desire to participate in a rise of gold or silver or any other commodity, there are excellent ETFs that allow you to do this but without the excessive leverage of futures contracts. Any broker can sell you these, an ETF, not a mutual fund, and can send you information on them. There are also agricultural ETFs.

A Note on Hedge Funds

To buy into a hedge fund you must be a "qualified" investor. That means you have to have more than one million dollars in liquid assets, not counting your home, and/or you must have an income of more than $300,000 per year for the past two or three years.

Even if you are a qualified investor, getting into a good hedge fund usually requires a capital infusion of more than $500,000 to $3 to 5 million. In any case 1) hedge funds are not regulated by the SEC and frequently take big risks with YOUR money, 2) management fees are usually very high, more than 2-3 per cent per year and 3)as noted above, although they do not participate in any losses, they take 20 per cent of any profits, off the top.   Thus they are rewarded for taking risks if they win and not penalized (much) if they lose.

Hedge funds are not for the small or medium sized investor.

Chapter 13: Bonds and Preferred Stocks.

Just a brief word on fixed income securities: Bonds are simply debt.   That is, if a company or a state , or a country wants to borrow money, the cheapest way is to go to the market place, declare they want to borrow money and how much, and ask around or check other types of debt to determine how much it will cost to borrow the money, the interest rate.   If they want to use the money for a long time before giving it back, the cost, (interest rate), will usually be higher than if they plan to pay it back in a short time.   If the borrower is a big, rich company, state, or country, and chances are very good that they will pay the money back in full and pay the interest on time, i.e., the risk that the lender will lose money is very low, they don't have to pay as high an interest rate as a small, new company with shaky credit, would. When the company, country, state, gets the money, it gives the lender a contract promising to give back the money on a certain date, and to pay a determined rate of interest, usually every six months.   This contract is called a bond and is transferable, i.e. it can be sold from one bond holder to another, in the market place. When the US government issues short term bonds, less than two years, they are called notes or bills, e.g. treasury (T) bills.   They do not pay interest periodically but pay interest when they are redeemed --paid off.   They are discounted, i.e. for a 1 year $10,000 T bill paying 5 per cent you will pay $9,500 on day one, but receive $10,000 one year later.

Bonds are usually issued in denominations of $1000, $5,000, $10,000 and into the millions; the price is discussed, and published as if the bond were for $100.   The price of the bond fluctuates with supply and demand though the amount of money the borrower pays periodically to the bond holder remains constant; hence the interest rate varies.   This is a little complicated.   If a company issues a bond for $1000 with a promise to pay back in 10 years and pays 6% interest when it is issued, the lender will get $60 per year for ten years and then will get his money, the principal, back.   If money is tight two years later, and the usual interest rate goes up to, say, 10 per cent, a new bond for $1000 would pay $100 per year to the bond buyer, the lender.   If the owner of the 6 per cent bond wanted to sell his bond that gives only 6 per cent per year, or $60 per year, no one would pay him $1000 to get only $60 per year. If he wanted to sell it, he would have to accept less money for it.   At first glance it seems he would only get $600 for the bond—then the new holder of the bond would be getting 10 per cent, ($60) for his money. It is not that simple, because in eight years (the 10 year bond is now 2 years old) he will get a full $1000. The bond, to pay 10% "to maturity" would probably sell for about $800. The current interest rate would be 60/800 or 7.5 per cent, and the additional $200 received at maturity, divided by the eight years to maturity, would be another $25/year.   So the total income per year would be $60 plus $25 or $85, which is an interest rate to maturity of 85/800 or 10.635%. This is an approximation, and the formula is somewhat different, because you are getting the additional $25 per year, the discounted amount of $200, only after waiting for eight years.   If the going interest rate goes down, say to 4%, the bond will sell for a higher amount, having a premium rather than a discount.   The price of the bond can be figured out similarly. It would be about $1120, with the new owner receiving $60 per year, about 5.36% of the $1120, as current income; the bond would be worth $15 less per year ($120/8 years) or lose about 1.3% per year so the bond would be paying about 4%, the current rate to maturity--again an approximation. Hence when you buy a bond you are guaranteed a set income per year, and that you will get your principal back in a set number of years; the value of the bond, if you want to sell it before it matures, will fluctuate with the interest rate, inverse to the interest rate. If the going interest rate goes down the sale price of the bond will go up; if the going interest rate goes up the sale value of the bond will go down.

So bonds provide stable income until they reach maturity, when you get all your initial money back. Hence they are considered "safe" and good investments for retirees, and others who need a stable income to maintain themselves. and who cannot afford to suffer the vagaries and uncertainties of common stocks in the marketplace.

A variant of bonds that trade like stocks and are fixed income securities are preferred stock. When a company wants to raise capital, instead of a bond, it might sell a preferred stock issue. This stock usually carries a dividend that is usually above the T bill percentage rate, and sometimes above the rate paid to their bond holders. It is called "preferred" because the dividend of the preferred stock must be paid before any dividends can be paid to the holders of the common stock. Thus, if a company has financial difficulties, it must cut its common stock dividend first before it cuts its preferred dividend.   If trouble persists, it may cut its preferred dividend.

If it is a cumulative preferred, it must later pay all the dividends it omitted before it can pay any dividends on its common stock. Bond holders always get their payments—by not paying the interest on its debt, the company is in default, which is next to bankruptcy.   If a company does become bankrupt, the first claim on the remaining assets goes to the bondholders, what is left goes to the preferred stockholders. Only what remains after the preferred stockholders are paid off goes to the common shareholders, usually very little if anything.

Preferred stock has a few advantages over bonds.   They are usually priced at $25 per share and are readily accessible.   They are fairly liquid and can be bought and sold readily like any other stock.   Although they are basically debt instruments, for tax purposes the payments are usually considered dividends and are taxed at only 20 per cent (2017) and not as interest income which is taxed as if it were ordinary income.

A word on taxes and bonds: Corporate bond interest is taxed as ordinary income.   There is no federal tax on municipal bonds and no state tax if the municipal bond is issued by the state you pay taxes to. If the municipal bond is from another state, for example, if you live in New Jersey and you have a New York state bond, you must pay New Jersey state income tax on the interest income from New York.   Federal bond, T bill and T note interest are taxed as regular income by the feds but are not taxed by the states. Be careful with municipal bonds, however.   Many are called "tax free" but are counted when you figure minimum tax and then will be taxed.

Briefly, "minimum tax" was initiated some years ago to enable the government to tax very rich people whose income was all in non-taxable entities. " Rich" used to be an annual income of about $150,000. Now, as inflation has raised the number of dollars that we receive with a decrease in the buying power of each dollar, many middle class workers are in the minimum tax bracket. Most accountants figure out the tax as if there were no minimum tax, and refigure the tax for minimum tax, adding back deductions for state income taxes, real estate taxes, some forms of depreciation, etcetera, and adding back the interest on some municipal bonds.   Tax on the new total, about 20%, is compared to the tax calculated as if there were no minimum tax, and you pay whichever is higher.   Thus although "tax free" bonds appear to generate more income because of the tax benefit, a 5 per cent municipal bond will effectively give about the same income as a

7.6 per cent taxable corporate bond if you are in the 35 per cent bracket—35 per cent of 7.6 per cent goes to the government.   If the municipal bond is "subject to minimum tax" and your income is higher than $200,000, you may get no tax benefit from that municipal bond.

The downside of preferred stock is twofold.   First, you do not benefit from any upside movement of the company's stock or of the company's success.   The dividend is fixed, never goes up, and could be cut if the company gets into deep trouble.   Secondly, you get only minimal benefit if the general interest rate goes down, but all of the downside if the general interest rate goes up. With a bond, if the general market interest rate goes down, your bond is worth more. Similarly, if the general market interest rate goes up the bond is worth less on the open market. With preferred stocks, if the interest rate goes up, your stock is worth less, but if interest rates go down, preferred stocks do not appreciate much because preferred stocks usually have a five year call provision that is at the discretion of the issuing company. Thus, if you own 100 shares of QRS preferred paying 7 per cent, if the general interest rate goes down to 5 per cent, i.e. the company can get money by issuing a preferred that has to pay only 5 per cent, it will call your stock at 5 years and pay back your original $2500 with possibly a $100 bonus. If, however, the going interest rate goes up to 8.5 per cent, i.e., the company would have to pay 8.5 per cent on any new preferred it issued, and your stock is now worth about $22 per share, it will not call it at five years and you are stuck with it for up to 30 years unless you want to sell and take the loss.

The conventional wisdom is that as you get older, and nearer to retirement, your investments should be mostly in fixed income securities. In fact there is a conventional formula: your age should be equal to the percentage of investments that are in fixed income entities. Thus at 35-years-old, you should have 65 per cent in stocks and 35 per cent in fixed income. At 50-years-old, 50-50 stocks and fixed income; at 65-years-old, 65 per cent in fixed, and 35 per cent in stocks, and so forth.

As with other pearls of conventional wisdom, this also has flaws. That is, we are and will continue to be for a long time, in an inflationary economy even though interest rates are low. Thus we can buy much less for $100 now than we could 10 years ago and in ten years we will be able to buy much less than we can for our $100 now. Thus, in order to maintain a stable standard of living, our income must continue to grow with inflation. As a rule of thumb, we should never take out more than 4 per cent of our investment capital per year, and should reinvest, or hold in the account any appreciation or income from the account in excess of

4 per cent.   The safest way to do this, I feel, is to invest in dividend paying stocks that produce products or services that are necessary and selling and thus will probably be in business in ten to fifteen years.   These stocks will grow with inflation and usually so will their dividends.   This growth is not necessarily linear, and is usually sporadic, but over the long run is predictable.   For stable income, I would hold some bonds and some of the preferreds— now mainly issued by banks—paying about 3-5 per cent.   For stable income, with upside potential with usual increases in dividends, I would consider the stocks in highly rated utilities, power companies, telephone companies, and gas companies that usually pay more than 4 per cent.

The conventional ways of achieving an ongoing reliable income have come up for reappraisal in the current environment of excessively low interest rates instituted in the last decade in an effort to get the economy growing again.   The theory was that if the interest rates were low enough more businesses would be encouraged to borrow, expand, create new jobs and grow the economy.   It did not work that way because the banks were unwilling to take chances and lend at the low interest rates and it became more and more difficult to get a loan.   Moreover whenever the fed tried to raise interest rates the investment markets have responded by dropping and this further depressed growth.

With the fed rates below 11/2% retirees and those on fixed
incomes have looked elsewhere; e.g., MLPs, REITs, and junk
bonds rather than safe government bonds for sources of income.

A Master Limited Partnership is an investment vehicle where
a company can raise capital by selling units that pay virtually all
the income (90%) of the partnership to the unit holders without the
company paying taxes on the income.   The unit holder (partner)
pays taxes on what he receives.   There are a large number of
master limited partnerships for petroleum drillers, pipelines,
refiners, etc. Because they must pass most of their profit directly
to the "partner" (owner of the shares), they usually give dividends
in excess of 5 per cent. Also, frequently, some of the income is not
taxed because it is depreciation, return of capital, etcetera.   Not
uncommonly, also, the dividends grow.   They are a bit annoying
at tax time; there are special forms that have to be filed by your
accountant, but for the most part, they are worth it.   Some
newsletters frequently suggest limited partnerships for income.
Skousen is one of them.

A large number of seniors have invested in MLPs and a lot have
lost money. It is necessary to be careful. A large number of gas
and oil drillers have used MLPs to raise the large amount of
working capital that they require to continue drilling . This is

because with fraccing and with horizontal drilling the resulting pools of oil or gas that they tap into are small and usually go dry in months to 1-2 years. Basically (simply) they drill into oil or gas saturated shale and explode a charge in the hole. This creates a cavity underground that fills with the petroleum from the shale. The oil or gas is then pumped out until the cavity is emptied. They then must repeat the process in a different hole. This is somewhat different from tapping into a lake of under-ground oil where you can pump out oil for years. Using this technique old oil wells that have gone dry can be made productive again. Horizontal drilling is similar. After a well is dry if you drill at the same under ground level horizontally (instead of going deeper); e.g., north or south you may drill into another pool of oil or gas. If this does not occur and if you have drilled into rock or shale containing oil or gas, you can fracc it—explode a charge and create a cavity that will free up the oil or gas so it can be pumped out. With the current decrease in the price of oil and gas, drillers have been unable to pay MLF dividends and many have decreased or stopped their payments and some have gone bankrupt. It is important at this time to avoid the MLPs of drillers unless you are sure they can continue to service their debt. Stick with the MLPs of refiners or pipeline companies It is unlikely that these companies who are not drillers or producers will cut their dividends.

REITs (Real Estate Investment Trust) are similar to MLPs in that 90% of the income passes directly to the holders of the units, and the company does not pay income taxes. The unit holders do. Over the past few years some of these REITs have also had problems and have decreased or discontinued their payouts. Those associated with residential real estate have done well and have continued to pay their distributions.   Those associated with malls or shopping centers have not fared as well partly due to the crushing effect that Amazon has had on retail facilities.

Seekers of increased fixed income in this environment have also been investing in "junk" bonds. These are bonds originated by companies that have a poor credit rating, bbb to C.   To get access to capital they must pay a relatively high multiple of the going T bill rate, typically significantly over 6%. These bonds are inherently risky. In addition to unreliable interest payments, a small percentage of these companies fail and there is lttle return of the principle amount of the bond.   You should check on the company yourself. Make sure that they have a product, a sales volume, and have a cash flow, and that they do not have excessive debt. Some years ago Milkin made money in junk bonds becasuse he felt that the price of these bonds was higher than appropriate for their risk. He was a very sophisticated investor. Remember the risk of losing your principle in these bonds is real and be careful if you invest in them.

Other than these instruments for income, as you near retirement age, you should invest in individual stocks that pay > 3 per cent dividends and that have a track record of increasing their dividend each year. Any brokerage you deal with, even discount brokers, can get you a list of these stocks that have a record of yearly dividend growth, and many of the market newsletters suggest excellent income portfolios. (e.g., Bryan Perry)

There is a variant of fixed income securities that is a hybrid between stocks and bonds. These are "convertible" bonds or convertible preferred stocks. By creating such a hybrid the issuer, the company that sells the security, can pay a lower interest rate than if there were no convertible provision, and he doesn't have to issue more shares immediately. Issuing more shares would raise capital, but would dilute the value of the outstanding shares and would decrease the apparent profit per share--more shares to divide the total profit of the company by. Convertible securities are beneficial for the buyer, that is, the lender, in that, first, he gets more income than is paid by the common stock dividend, and secondly, he can participate in a large upside movement of the stock. Moreover, the instrument has a floor below which it will not fall because of the interest payout, a floor that he would not have if he bought the stock outright. The downside is that the payout is less than for a conventional bond or preferred stock. The upside movement in the value of the instrument is not as great as if he bought the common stock, and to a great extent, if the stock goes down, the convertible equity will also go down though not by as much as if he held the common stock.

The best explanation is a hypothetical example:

QRS Company stock is selling for $20 per share. They need money, for example, ten million dollars, but don't want to pay the going rate of 8 percent for it. They don't want to issue and sell more common stock outright because they do not want to dilute their stock right away. If they add 20 per cent more stock, their earnings per share would go down by about 17 per cent and their share price might go down.

QRS issues a twenty year convertible bond: Each $1000 bond is convertible into 40 shares of QRS common stock, and they pay interest of 6 per cent per year. Thus, the bond is not worth converting into common stock now; it is worth converting when the common stock trades for more than $25 per share. This provision, to allow the bondholder to participate in the upside potential of the stock, costs the bond-buyer 2 per cent/year; the ability to not dilute the stock costs the borrower the 6 per cent per year.   If the stock goes up, the value of the bond will go up by $40 per one dollar advance in stock price beyond $25.   At $30 per share, the $1000 bond would be worth over $1200.   If the stock were to go down to $12 per share, the convertible provision would not be of much value, but the bond would only drop to about $830 ($60/year income= 7.23 per cent plus $8.50 per year times 20 years equals 7.23 per cent plus .85 per cent per year equals current income plus increasing value per year or about 8 per cent income to maturity.)   So there is a floor on the value of the bond. Convertible preferreds work similarly.

Addendum Chapter: Living in Interesting Times.

2008 has been an extraordinary year—not in a good way.

The causes for the dramatic market decline and the difficult economy are complicated, convoluted, multiple and complex. It is not possible to lay blame and it is not possible to simplify what has been going on but I will try.

Basically, what has occurred is the result of a crisis of confidence and trust in the economic structure and in financial systems that has lead to a drying up of available credit. Although my take on it may be simplified and not entirely accurate I will try to explain the events as I see them.

The stress to the system started with housing. Traditionally, the prospective buyer of a house goes to the bank for a mortgage loan. The banker, who had a limited amount of the bank's money to lend, evaluates the buyer's finances to ensure that he could pay the monthly interest, amortization and taxes, and that he could repay the loan. After carefully evaluating the house--- that would be collateral for the loan --- he would insist that the buyer put up at least 25% of the value of the house as a down payment, and the bank would lend 75% or less, of the houses value, with 100% of the house as collateral. Given that the banker is lending the banks money, he is being careful not to risk losing it. The banks profit is the difference between the low interest rate given to depositors for use of their money, short term interest rate, and the higher interest paid by the mortgage holder, long term interest rate. The important aspect is that it is the banks money, it is finite, and the banker is thorough.

To make evaluation of housing easier, banks would determine areas of their city or county where they would not lend, drawing red lines on a map to easily identify areas where housing values were low or unstable. Because these areas were usually in poor neighborhoods, where the majority of the buyers were members of minority groups, such redlining was declared illegal in the late 1970's under former US President Jimmy Carter and any banker caught redlining was subjected to a large fine. As a result, evaluation of housing was less diligent. To make it easier on the banks, however, the feds established a mechanism, (FNMA, fanny mae), whereby, after loaning the money the bank could sell the mortgage to the feds and get the money they lent back and continue to get a small fee for servicing and administering the mortgage. Initially the mortgage to be sold to the feds had to be meticulously obtained and safe.

In the 1990's, President Clinton insisted that the American dream of home ownership be opened to more people and loosened the criteria for Fanny Mae and Freddy Mack, a similar agency to FNMA. This made it easier to lay off loans to the fed and encouraged the banks to be less conservative regarding mortgages. In the early part of this century with the double whammy of the bursting of the Dot Com bubble followed by the 9/11 terrorist attack, to head off a recession, Greenspan lowered interest rates markedly and the floodgates for mortgages opened wide.

Now the banks had no qualms about giving mortgages to whomever applied, whether they were credit worthy or not, and at whatever the price of the house. It was no longer their money that was being loaned. They immediately got the money back from the feds and would keep any fees associated with placing the mortgage and collecting the payments.   Moreover, now the business of Fanny and Freddy looked so good that more private investors got involved. They found they could lend their money for mortgages and could get it back almost immediately, not by going to the feds but by packaging large numbers of these mortgages into bonds. The bonds were backed by the interest paid by the homeowners on their mortgages; the bonds were rated as per the name of the packager, large banks, not by the actual creditworthiness of the homeowners and their mortgages.   Thus, bonds sold by banks were rated as safe because the banks were prestigious.   The packaging banks got the relatively high interest paid by the mortgage holders, they kept a lot of it but were still able to give a generous interest rate to the bond buyers who were getting what appeared to be a safe highly rated bond with a coupon higher than other bonds similarly rated. Everyone, it appears, was fat and happy.

Meanwhile the banks were lending first mortgages wildly with numerous crazy gimmicks that made them ridiculously unsafe to the lender. For instance, buyers required:

no down payments

no need for a buyer to prove that he had a stable income and could afford the mortgage, called no documentation loans

no proper appraisal of the property

They were given low initial rates for the first few years with higher rates later, interest only mortgages with no amortization, i.e. no paying down of the mortgage as part of the monthly payment, adjustable rate mortgages that lead to higher payments if interest rates increase. People who could really not afford to buy a house were encouraged to do so. Part of this was predicated on the belief that the value of the house would always go up. Even worse was the proliferation of second mortgages, more palatably called, home equity loans. As the value of his house went up the homeowner could borrow more money using the appreciation of the house value as collateral. Meanwhile more and more banks and investment companies and hedge funds were buying the bonds as safe investments that were really packages of questionable high risk mortgages.

Then a secondary industry appeared. Someone got the bright idea to insure the value and the interest payments of these bonds and some sophisticated derivatives of these bond insurance vehicles, credit default swaps were developed.   It was very complicated.

But simply put, the bond holder or issuer paid a yearly premium to the insurer.   If the bond issuer paid its interest payments on time, the insurer pocketed the premium as profit.   If he didn't pay, the bond was in default and the insurer would take the bond and pay to the bondholder the difference between the face value of the bond and the value of the defaulted bond.   The rates for this insurance were inappropriately low because by history, bonds sold by these large banks and other institutions that were as highly rated as these bonds were (inappropriately), rarely defaulted.   If the bonds had been rated appropriately no one would have insured them, certainly not at these low premium rates.   The insurer was taking a much higher risk than he thought he was. Moreover, since it seemed such a low risk investment, financial institutions were selling credit default swaps to any buyers, whether they owned the bonds or not.   That is, the credit default swap buyer was betting that the bond would default and he would then get the difference between the face value of the bond and the market price of the bond, and the insurer was betting that the bond would not default and he would pocket the premium.   This is like buying life insurance on someone else's life, betting that he will die, or buying hurricane insurance on someone else's house.

A credit swap is a sophisticated financial instrument originally created to exchange a variable interest income into a fixed interest income.   This is better understood by citing an example.

Mr. Brown lends $100,000 to Mr. Jones and gets an interest rate that is 3% above LIBOR (the London interbank overnight rate that is constantly changing, similar to the US interbank lending rate).   Initially LIBOR is 5% so Mr. Jones is paying Mr. Brown $8000/year. When LIBOR goes up, Mr. Brown will get more interest; if LIBOR goes down he will get less interest. But he needs a steady income of $8000/year. Mr. Smith comes around and says I am willing to gamble that LIBOR will go up.   I will take your variable interest risk and give you 8% per year, and if the interest rate goes down, I will pay you the difference between the 8% and the lower interest rate. However, if the interest rate goes up, you must pay me the difference between the higher interest rate and the 8% that I am guaranteeing to you.   Mr. Brown is happy because he is guaranteed his $8000/year, and Mr. Smith is happy because he has a chance to make a lot of money if LIBOR goes up.

Currency swaps work similarly. They are ways to change a variable income into a fixed income. With credit default swaps, the insurer is taking the risk of default, which should occur rarely, for a premium from the bondholder who does not want to risk the loss of his principal.

This entire system was based on the principle that housing prices would always go up, that houses could always be sold promptly. So a homeowner who lost his income and could not keep up with the payments could sell his house without having a foreclosure, and that all these high risk mortgages would always have their interest paid, so the issuers of bond insurance or credit default swaps would only rarely be required to pay for a failing bond.

Because these bonds were thought to be safe and because they paid a generous interest rate and because many of them were "insured", a lot of banks, pension funds, and hedge funds purchased them for their own portfolios. They were carried on their books as assets, making up a large percent of the net worth of some institutions. Also, many institutions were insuring these bonds to make the premium, and were also playing the credit default swap game selling insurance to individuals who did not own the bonds, but who were gambling that the bonds would default.

By mid 2007, well after the dot com bubble burst and well
after the 9/11 attacks, the economy had recovered, the stock market
(except for NASDAQ) had returned to almost the 1999-2000 level,
the prime interest rate also recovered and was back up to about
4.5%.

At this 4.5% level of the prime rate, the price (interest rate) of
mortgages also had increased so that it was not as easy to fund the
buying of a house. Moreover, homeowners with adjustable rate
mortgages, (ARMS), suddenly found their monthly payments
rising above their ability to comfortably pay the now higher
monthly rate. In addition, the speculators who were flipping
houses suddenly found they could not flip the houses they had
bought. A house flipper is dependent on consistently rising prices
for houses.   For example, he buys a house for $400,000, holds it
for a year and sells it for $550,000.   He puts up $50,000 (or less)
and takes a loan at 6% (or less) for the rest.   Hence the year of
holding costs $21,000 plus taxes, e.g. $15,000.   When he sells the
house for $550,000 he repays the $350,000 loan and ends up with
$550,000 minus $350,000 minus $21,000 interest, minus $15,000
taxes, or $164,000. Thus, his $50,000 investment has grown by
228%. Not bad for one year. However, if the speculator cannot
sell the house, he cannot make his profit; also he has to continue

paying the loan interest and the property tax. If the property does not go up as much as he expects, he will eventually sell for a lesser profit, or eventually he will sell for no profit and even take a small loss, and eventually he will sell taking a large loss to end the ongoing costs of ownership.

Hence there are more and more houses on the market. (Builders who build houses on spec also add to this oversupply.) And there are fewer buyers because by now mortgage rates are up and fewer people can afford to buy.

If there is more inventory of houses (excess supply) than house buyers (less demand) prices go down. With the decrease in housing prices the whole house of cards began to topple and the fabric based on higher and higher house values began to unravel.

It appears that first a few homeowners were not able to make their payments and then the interest on the bonds was not paid. This was OK because the insurers of the bonds paid off on their credit default swaps. But then the banks and hedge funds and financial institutions such as pension funds that held the bonds began to worry about the reliability of their bonds, and began to look at the true value of their bonds. A bond is only worth what someone is willing to pay for it. Consequently, no one felt they could trust what these bonds were worth and no one wanted to buy them. If there is no market for these bonds they theoretically have no value (even though most of these bonds continued to pay their usual interest).   On the principle of mark to market, suddenly a hedge fund or a bank that had total assets of 2 billion dollars with 1.25 billion face value mortgage backed bonds on Monday, on Tuesday would have a net asset value of 0.75 billion because the 1.25 billion bond asset was now worth zero because there was no market for the bonds, and by the principle of mark to market, they must be carried as worth zero.   Moreover, by law, a bank must maintain net assets of a certain percentage of its depositors equity and if assets go down, the bank is insolvent and must cease to exist.   A decrease in the net asset value of hedge funds and also other businesses, can cause the loans that they have borrowed to be called.   For instance, if the net asset value of a fund is $500 million dollars, the fund can borrow another 200 million, but the loan contract states that if their net asset value drops below 300 million, they must immediately repay the loan--- similar to a margin call. If they don't repay the loan, they are in default, and must declare bankruptcy.   In such a situation, these banks and hedge funds and other businesses sell whatever assets they own. They sell any stocks they own: more sellers of stocks than buyers leads inevitably to a decrease in stock prices and the > 50 percent precipitous price drop we saw in shares in many companies that were solvent, making profits, and basically solid investments in 2008. Moreover, these banks and funds squeeze anyone that owes them money to pay it back. To survive they start cutting their costs of doing business—cutting overhead. The quickest way to do this is to fire people and cut payroll. When enough firms do this there is suddenly a worrisome increase in unemployment.

What is worse though , and more serious, and what has really thrown a monkey wrench in the system, is that when the net asset value of a bank is suddenly declared to have dropped significantly, the bank stops lending and raises its interest rates, especially on credit cards, to recapitalize itself.

If banks stop, or slow down lending, all commerce slows or stops. A case in point: no lending, or less lending and almost no one buy cars. At about $20-30,000 for the average car, almost everyone must get a car loan or a lease, which is a form of loan. There is no money for mortgages so home sales and purchases dry up. There is no lending to small businesses to keep cash flow steady during slow periods to fund payroll; small businesses do not expand and add workers, and they may fire people to cut their overhead. Increased credit card interest leads to less spending. Less spending, leads to less consumption, which in turn leads to less production and personnel layoffs, Consequently, there is higher unemployment followed by deflation, recession and finally to depression.

Meanwhile defaults in mortgage payments increase, and more credit default swap insurers cannot fulfill their contracts and get in deep trouble, for example, AIG. Companies with net asset value below their liability level, cannot get the day to day loans that keep them liquid because no one knows what they are worth, and whether they will repay, go under (Lehman Bros) or almost go under (Citigroup). Car companies cannot sell cars without readily available credit, so they almost go under or close factories or go into hibernation (Chrysler). Foreign car makers pull back to their own country, closing US plants (Nissan) or canceling new factory building in the US (BMW). All this leads to more unemployment, decreased spending, deflation and the recession that has occurred.

In addition, even among those who continue to have their jobs and continue to have an income (only about 8% are unemployed or, looked the other way more than 90% of the workers remain employed) some get less overtime but even if income is unchanged they spend less—for three reasons.

    1) the main reason; They feel less rich, because they know the value of their home has decreased by about 30%. And their retirement nest egg, 401K or IRA has decreased by 30-50%

because these funds are largely invested in stocks and bonds (via mutual funds and pension funds.)

2) Everyone worries about losing his job or that a member of his family, a son, daughter, sister, brother, parent, might lose his job and he may have to help them financially.

3) They feel that if they postpone buying, prices will probably go down; they do not spend now.   This leads to further deflation because, yes, prices will come down.   But store owners will have to cut their overhead to stay in business; they will fire workers and squeeze their suppliers.   Their suppliers, the manufacturers, must get rid of inventory so they will cut the prices to the stores. But to stay in business they will cut overhead by firing workers, by cutting production and by squeezing their subcontractors and raw material suppliers.

For example, the consumer anticipating lower prices does not buy the shirt now but elects to wait.   The store owner eventually sells the shirt for 50% off; gets rid of 30% of his sales staff and squeezes the shirt manufacturer, who, to move his inventory, cuts his price by 50%; to stay in business he cuts production and fires half of his factory workers. He also squeezes the companies who supply his buttons and his cloth and his thread and his needles and his sewing machines.

Each of these companies do the same thing and deflation leads to worse and worse economic conditions.

This analysis is not completely accurate but it gives a general picture of what has happened or begun to happen in 2008.   Maybe it could have been avoided if there was no fed interference in banking that encouraged aggressive mortgage lending by buying the mortgages by Fanny Mae and Freddy Mac so fewer risky mortgages would have been issued. (But fewer people would be able to enjoy home ownership). Perhaps if there had been more regulation, insurance companies would not have been allowed to insure bonds that were risky without having sufficient reserves to deal with an unforeseen catastrophe.   Perhaps if the rating agencies were better regulated, they would have been more diligent and not rated the mortgage collateralized bonds inappropriately high so not so many would have been sold or insured.   Perhaps if Greenspan had not cut the interest rates so excessively after 9/11, or had re-raised the interest rates earlier, the housing bubble with rapidly rising home prices would not have occurred, and hence would not have burst.   Perhaps if gimmicky mortgages had not been allowed (ARM's, no down payment loans, or no amortization loans) fewer houses would be in foreclosure, house flipping would have been less profitable and hence not done and also, fewer houses would have been built on speculation.   Perhaps if the fed had acted earlier and better, the recession could have been prevented, or at least made less painful.   Perhaps if Lehman Brothers had not been allowed to go under all of this could have been avoided.

Why was Lehman Brothers bankruptcy so critical? Lehman Bros was an important market maker for mortgage collateralized bonds and for the credit default swaps.   The market maker is the middle man who is always available to buy a security from anyone who wants to sell and always has some inventory of securities to sell to anyone who wants to buy.   On the stock exchange, they are called specialists.   They essentially set the prices; they do this as they stabilize their inventory.   Hence, if their inventory of securities gets low they will charge more to the buyer and to replace their inventory they will pay more to the seller.   If their inventory gets too large, they will sell it off at a lower price to a buyer and will buy less, or only at a lesser price from those who want to sell. The market maker must be cognizant of the fluctuation of prices, and be very nimble to maintain his inventory from getting too small or too large, doing this by changing the prices to buyers and sellers rapidly and accurately.

Apparently when there were fewer buyers for the mortgage collateralized bonds the market maker, Lehman Bros., was stuck with a large inventory that they could not sell, the value of the bonds in the inventory went down much below their cost, and the asset value of the bonds decreased markedly (or by mark to market was essentially zero) and suddenly Lehman Brothers was undercapitalized. They also held an unknown amount of liability as the seller of credit default swaps. This question as to their net worth made it difficult for them to get the overnight loans they needed to stay liquid, solvent and in business.   If an investment bank is undercapitalized, it is insolvent, they must declare bankruptcy and must cease to exist. Since Lehman had apparently made a lot of money in the past on these mortgage collateralized bonds and their executives had extracted large bonuses, and since they also played a role that was very profitable in creating and marketing credit default swaps, it was felt that it was poetic justice to let them go under and it would have posed a "moral hazard" to bail them out, i.e. reward or rescue the bad guys. The feds chose to let them go belly up. They were also felt to be small enough that their bankruptcy would not upset the system excessively. Did the fact that Goldman Sachs is a major competitor of Lehman Brothers and that the head of treasury was a former, and probably future partner at Goldman Sachs play a role in choosing Lehman to be the punished example to other financial institutions? We will never know.

Nevertheless, this was a major mistake and in the future it will be credited as being the major catastrophe that almost (?) destroyed the economy.   Because it killed confidence in the system.   The feds, probably for low cost, could have guaranteed their credit so they could stay in business until valuation of their "questionable" assets could be more fairly determined.   Almost immediately, over the next few weeks the stock market dropped another 30%.   It was now assumed that the mortgage collateralized bonds had no value, although most of these bonds continued to pay their usual interest. The asset value and net worth of many banks and investment and hedge funds in the United States tanked and many were theoretically bankrupt, or near bankrupt.   It turned out that many financial institutions in Europe, Asia and Iceland and throughout the world, and even the treasuries of foreign governments lost serious asset value because they held these unmarketable bonds—originally thought to be safe and originally bought to get their slightly higher yield.   And institutions and even local governments who were inadvertently the sellers of these presumed very safe credit default swaps to earn the premiums found themselves at risk for great losses.

Then the next near catastrophe occurred, that was fortunately averted. Holders of Fanny Mae and Freddie Mac bonds- including many foreign banks and the central banks of many countries began to question the safety of these bonds. In reality all Fanny and Freddy bonds are mortgage collateral obligation bonds. (Remember, it was Fanny and Freddy that first started buying mortgages from banks and selling bonds that were collateralized by these mortgages with the source of the interest payments being the mortgage payments paid by the homeowners.) Holders of these bonds suddenly read the fine print and realized that unlike treasury bonds and T-bills, Fanny and Freddy paper was **not** backed by the full faith and credit of the US government. And they started to sell them. Realizing that this could start a slide that could result in a worldwide deep recession, the fed wisely declared that they would back these bonds in full and staved off a really major debacle. (The next event would probably been a run on the dollar, in the form of all the central banks around the world dumping T-Bills—e.g. China and Japan hold T bills worth more than all the US currency in circulation and almost worth more than the US GDP for one year.)

But the demise of Lehman Brothers still had a catastrophic effect.   With major disruption of the usual market for their mortgage collateralized bonds, the net asset value of banks went through the floor and major banks were threatened with bankruptcy.   Treasury arranged a rapid bailout where they said the fed would buy these bonds and create a market for them. This did not work well, possibly because the banks did not want to sell because it would force them to take a documented loss, not just a paper loss in their net asset value, or for other reasons.   Because this loss due to this decrease in marketability of their bonds was world-wide, the central banks of other governments had to deal with it.   Britains central bank had the best idea.   Rather than buy these toxic bonds they instead injected capital into a bank that was about to go under because of its exposure to US mortgage collateralized bonds. This worked, stopped a run on the bank, and staved off bankruptcy.

In the United States, Citibank was on the verge of bankruptcy, its stock had dropped from the 60's to low single digits. Even with an injection of capital from Warren Buffet and from the Arabian prince who already owned a large percentage of the bank, things were still dicey.   Wachovia was taken over by Wells Fargo in a fire sale, and Washington Mutual was virtually given to J P Morgan Chase.   The fed watched what was happening in Britain, saw that it was good, and started injecting capital into banks.   Because they did not want to precipitate a run on a bank (where all depositors want their money—now), by identifying which banks were in trouble, they gave every large bank an infusion of capital. This has, sort of, worked—so far.

When a bank is undercapitalized, the first thing it does (after cutting its overhead by firing personnel) is to stop giving loans or at least to slow down the making of loans.   It also raises its interest rates, which all the banks have done.   By injecting capital into banks, the hope was that this would free up credit and get the economy going again.   Unfortunately, to get money into the system fast with no arguments,   the feds are giving all this taxpayers money to the banks with no strings attached so they have **not** freed up credit much and continue to pay their executives large salaries and disgustingly high bonuses. (They really don't deserve high bonuses for doing such a lousy job that they have to be bailed out by the feds).

Of course this has angered a lot of taxpayers.   But it must be remembered that the banks and the banking system are a utility, much like water, electric power and light, the railway system, and the telephone system.   In order for the economy and the United States society to function we need banks as much as electricity. No banks, equals no credit. No credit means no house or car sales and a serious clamp on small business as discussed earlier. We might want to punish the individuals who have run the banks so badly, but we must not destroy the banking system. A few banks can be allowed to fail but the system (which means the big banks) must survive, or we all are in deep trouble.

Appropriately, the fed has not been sitting still and has been somewhat proactive.   So far in order to try to heal the system the fed has, first, created a (+/-) market for troubled securities. Secondly, by bailing out and recapitalizing the banks, they have tried to bring back credit into the system with mixed success. Thirdly, they have lowered the discount rate to 0.25% so any bank can borrow money from the fed, essentially paying no interest for it, the idea being that they should lend it easily at low rates and make money for the bank while jump starting the credit system. This has not worked yet. (I was angered to hear lately that Citibank is raising its credit card rates for the best borrowers from 9.9% to 14.9%/year—will this stimulate the consumer to buy???). Fourth, the fed is beginning to bail out specific industries, for example, the auto makers, in order to prevent a surge in unemployment as auto factories and the factories of their many suppliers go under.

Fifth, the fed has been broadening the definition of "bank" so that financial companies such as CIT, Goldman Sachs, and now even GMAC (an important source of General Motors car loans) can borrow directly from them.

The other tool to get the economy back on its feet is to give people money to spend. Bush did this in the spring of 2008 with some temporary benefit with a large tax rebate. The effect was positive but it was short-lived. President Obama is promising to throw money into the economy by creating jobs, funding projects to redo the aging infrastructure, repairing and replacing roads and bridges and water systems, etcetera, to put money into the hands of consumers and hence, energize the economy. A consumer who has money and spends it will eat in restaurants-- providing employment and money to restaurant workers--- will buy clothes (providing employment and money to store employees, to employees of the clothes manufacturers and their suppliers, to trucking companies who transport all the stuff and to all the employees of service companies that provide services to the workers who can now afford to purchase them) and will buy a television set, a car, a new home, etcetera, etcetera.   This is called the multiplier effect of money that is spent in the system.

All of these mechanisms, and techniques, many of which I don't know about, and methods yet to be devised, will eventually be effective and the United States and the world economy will survive and prosper. I have great faith in the ingenuity of the American businessman, the American banks and the federal government to get us through this difficult period.

(Note: this analysis is based on my interpretation of what I have read in my newsletters (Dessauer's has been especially useful re housing), the Wall Street Journal, and other publications, and what I have learned from financial TV and radio commentators.   It is probably a gross oversimplification of what has occurred, and I take full responsibility for its inaccuracies.)

As investors with a small (or large) amount of discretionary capital, what do we do now?

First and foremost, we **will** pull out of this mess and the US economy will recover.

Secondly, all of the techniques and methods that involve the fed, involve the massive creation of money and injection of this new money into the economy.

More money in the economy eventually results in higher prices and inflation. If there is a finite amount of goods available, and an increasing number of dollars, the price of the good inevitably goes up. If a company produces a product that people want or need, the consumer will purchase the product and if he has money he will not be reluctant to pay a higher price for it. The producing company will make more profit, the amount it pays in dividends will go up and the stock price will rise. This may not occur linearly with a gradual rise in share price; it will occur sporadically. There may be periods when the stock price may decrease because the cost to produce the product—labor and raw materials—may go up before the price of the product goes up; eventually the price of the product and of the stock will appreciate. So inflation will eventually result in higher stock prices.

Thirdly, in times of great turbulence when the stock market goes down, as is current, the lowering tide lowers all ships. A great number of stocks that were overvalued have come down markedly; also a number of stocks that were not overvalued have also come down, in many cases, excessively. As mentioned before, when banks have to increase their liquid assets, when mutual funds have to generate cash to fund withdrawals, and when hedge funds and individuals have to meet margin calls, they sell whatever is salable, including shares in good companies that they would prefer to keep, and the price of these stocks plummet along with the lesser quality companies.   Hence, there are a great many stocks that by any form of evaluation are going for bargain prices.   Thus, many good stocks are selling for prices that are below book value or replacement value, with historically low price to earnings ratios and that are going for just over the amount of cash the companies are holding.   Exchange traded funds (ETF's) and especially closed end funds are selling at steep discounts to their net asset value; i.e., you can buy one dollars worth of stock for 80-90 cents or less.   Many good stocks are paying dividends in excess of 5 percent.   As noted by many of my newsletter writers, this may be the buying opportunity of our lifetime.

On the other hand, this may be the pause before there is a further precipitous drop in the market.

If this recession is similar to the recessions we have experienced since World War II, a drop of 40-50% is the bottom, and we are there now.   If this is like the early thirties, however, we may go down to about 20% of the peak, meaning prices could drop by another 60% of their current prices.

Which is it? Regardless of how confident the prognosticator or how cogent his reasoning, no one knows for sure. Many of the excellent stock pickers who write the newsletters I have used have not been as successful as they had been. Many of the stocks they have suggested have been stopped out with 25-40% losses or remain in their portfolios carrying huge losses, the rationale being that these stocks are so low now that they are phenomenal buys and should not be sold at this time, but, instead, should be bought.

So what does one do? Do we sit on cash and wait for the **real** (?) bottom, which may occur later, before we invest? Or do we jump in and take advantage of these historically low prices and low valuations and risk the possibility of trying to catch a falling knife and risk further losses? Do we throw in the towel and sell everything and sit on cash until the market really recovers and goes up at least 15-20% from here, and possibly miss the bottom?

There is no good answer, but in the spirit of the way I do things, I have learned that no one is correct all of the time; almost every one is correct some of the time. Hence I have tended to be flexible, to compromise a bit, and to not bet the farm on any specific outcome.

1) Sell when the market letters say sell.

2) Sell a portion of the shares if you have large profits, e.g. >50%, in any company; keep your initial chip in the stock and use the profits to bottom fish.

3) Maintain enough cash to carry you for at least 3 months without income, in case you lose your job.

4) If you have discretionary capital left over divide it into four parts.

Invest the first 25% now. If the market goes up by 20% from when you invested the first quarter of your discretionary capital or if it goes down by 25%, invest the next quarter. If neither event occurs by three months, invest the second quarter. Use the same schedule after you invest the second quarter, investing the third quarter if the market goes up 20% or down by 25% from there or after three months, whichever comes first. The fourth quarter should be allocated similarly.

5) Readjust the size of your chip so that you have 6-10 chips in each 25% of your discretionary capital.

6) Follow the suggestions of a good newsletter, for example, Navalier, Band, Young, Skousen, Oxford Club, Leeb,

Cabot, Morningstar, or Dow Theory. But be sure to meticulously maintain a stop loss (mental) value of 25-30% with these new stocks you buy, selling them immediately if they reach that value.

7)   If you want to go it alone without a newsletter, the least risky way is:

A) Buy only stocks that give > 5% dividend and only if the estimated earnings for the next year are > 1.6 x the dividend payout. This data is readily available in Barrons.

B)   Buy only stocks that have names that you recognize.

C)   Buy only stocks that have fallen 30-50% in the past year.

D)   Buy utilities but only if they yield >6.5% and the estimated earnings for next year exceed the payout by 60% or greater (as above.)

E)   Buy only stocks in companies that you feel will be in business in 5 years regardless of the state of the economy, such as foods (Sysco, Heinz), low price restaurants (MacDonalds, Yum brands), defense (Raytheon, General Dynamics), consumer staples (Proctor and Gamble, Kimberly Clark), cheap end retailers (Walmart, TJX), very strong retailers (Tiffany, Abercrombie and Fitch, Nordstroms), utilities (Verizon, Duke Power, Con Edison).

F) Put only one chip in each of these stocks and watch closely re sell stop orders.

G) Another ploy that is more of a gamble: put one chip into any stock in the NYSE that you had held in the past 2 years (that you may have been stopped out of) that is selling for less than $8.00 and gives a dividend of greater than 4.0%. Again, observe the stops at 25-30% and only one chip in each.

H) Another ploy- one chip in each master limited partnership that is giving > 10% yield (pipeline, energy, water MLP's) that has been suggested by any newsletter in the past year and that has dropped by >50%.

I) Consider a crapshoot at the midlevel capital companies such as Gladstone, GDF, AOD that are giving 10-20% dividend yields. Only one chip in each, observe stop loss.

J) For income, consider preferreds issued by stable companies that are discounted such that the current yield is >10%. (bank preferreds are ok here if in very big banks, such as Bank of America, Wells Fargo, JP Morgan Chase, Bank of New York-Mellon.)

K) Take a position with at least 4 chips in a gold ETF and a gold mining stock such as Barrick.

In any case, make sure that the money you invest is not money you may need soon. Full recovery may not occur for >2-4 years and you must be able to hold (observing stop losses, however.) Try to pick only companies that are likely to survive more than 5 years; you will probably have one or two negative surprises, however. And stick with dividend paying stocks so holding for a long time will not be too painful. Expect that at least one in three stocks will decrease or suspend its dividend in the next 2 years. Invest only one or two chips in each stock; you will be diversified and you will survive a few negative surprises.

Remember, the United States is very resilient and this severe recession will also pass. Don't be afraid to invest, but do it with patience, caution, discipline (stop losses) and optimism. By 5 years your investments should be up by a factor of 2-4X.

Second Addendum

I have just finished rereading the first edition of "A Physician's Prescription For Successful Investing" that was published in 2009 and have updated the current newsletters and have added others.

The basic principles have not changed much. First, buy advice in the form of investment newsletters and use it. Try to take all of the advice, some, about 1/3 will be excellent and rewards will be >150-300 %. About 20% of the advice will be very bad and the stocks will plummet and may disappear. The remaining 5 of 10 will go up a bit or down a bit but will survive and most will thrive modestly. It is just that we do not which suggestions will do what. If we follow a discipline of paring the losers as soon as they go down by 30-35% and continuing to hold the others we will greatly succeed. If possible, try to buy mainly stocks that give 2-5% dividends so you can withstand periods of minimal activity. If you follow the advice of any of the listed newsletters you will end up diversified and you will be able to survive a sudden down turn.

The section on "Bad Advice" remains as pertinent as it was 10 years ago. Read it and consider it seriously

The section on mutual funds, options, futures and bonds are just as true as 10 years ago, if anything, more-so I have expanded the sections on ETFs and closed end funds and have expanded the options section to consider 2 of the current dangerous suggestions on how to get wealthy fast. Most players continue to be losers unless they sell only covered calls or are exceptionally lucky doing other maneuvers, including risky put sales. The section on bonds and fixed income securities has been expanded in view of the current low interest environment we have endured since 2009 and MLPs, REITs, and junk bonds are covered in more detail.

The strategies in the discussion of the economy in the first addendum chapter that were put into effect during the governments response to the severe recession of the 2008-2010 period have served to stabilize the economy though much of it has served to just kick the can down the road.   We continue to suffer the collateral damage of the techniques used: The interest rates have remained abnormally low, <1-2%, such that those living on fixed income (mainly retirees) have to invest in less than very safe non-government bonds.   The federal reserve has been afraid to raise interest rate because of the fragility of the economy.   The national debt has grown enormously because of the feds easing and creating money by buying bonds.   The yearly national budget contains an ever increasing burden of servicing the debt such that any increase in the interest rate would result in cutting almost all national spending except for defense and paying interest on the debt. Meanwhile the low interest rate has not served to stimulate the economy sufficiently and negative interest rates are being considered. (The "saver" pays a fee to the bank--negative interest-- on his deposits).   A corollary of negative interest rates is the doing away with cash, otherwise it would be cheaper to keep a mattress full of cash rather than have a savings account.   The hope would be that rather than lose money in a savings account the saver would spend money on things or investments and thereby stimulate the economy. It seems ridiculous, but some countries (e.g. Switzerland) have instituted negative interest bank accounts. The reason money has been created by the fed is to stimulate modest inflation. It has not worked and with all the money created the inflation rate stubbornly remains below 2%, the feds target rate.

With all of the stimulation of the economy growth has been elusive and modest at best. The nominal unemployment rate has come down nicely to about 4.5% and appears reasonable. The problem is that the jobs available are not as good or as well-paying as during the heyday of US manufacturing, and the number of workers who have quit looking for work has gone up so the unemployment number is unreliable. (The unemployment rate theoretically is the number of workers looking for work divided by the total number of those working and those not employed. Actually it is the number seeking unemployment insurance payments over the number working. After a set period of time of not working the unemployed worker does not get more benefits and does not count in the statistics.) Thus the unemployment rate may go down, not because more workers have found jobs but because more workers have left the work force. Moreover, the jobs available may not be full time. Employers have learned that if their workers work less than 30 hours/week they do not have to provide health insurance. Also the jobs available are usually in service industries and don't pay as well as the old manufacturing jobs.

In addition, the power of unions has been markedly diminished so US workers do not get paid as well. This is largely due to the globalization of the work force. Labor in many countries, especially in Asia but also in South and Central America are paid much less than US workers and large employers can move their point of manufacturing to the countries that require them to pay the least for their labor force. Thus over the past decade most manufacturing jobs which used to pay handsomely have left the US and there are large areas of the country where meaningful well-paying jobs are scarce. Our politicians have been unable to turn this around. This lack of well- paying jobs was much of the reason that Trump was able to destroy 16 republican contenders and was able to handily defeat Hillary Clinton. Except for the fringe of east and west coastal states, Trump took almost the rest of the country. The vast majority of mid US citizens were fed up with the promises with no follow-through from professional politicians and wanted a change, virtually any type of change from the pro to a novice who thought he could be effective. We are currently learning that there are skills that the professional politician learns as he gets elected to and serves in numerous offices before he becomes president. Without these skills, regardless of his intentions, he has difficulty getting anything done and defaults to trying to be dictatorial, bombastic, bullying, insulting and generally embarrassing as he tries to achieve his very reasonable goals. Most of us hope Trump can learn quickly on the job and become effective. It would be tragic if he were to be impeached, were to resign, or were to somehow be removed for incompetence. The things he wants to do need doing---- straighten out the healthcare debacle, strengthen our southern border, stop losing jobs to other countries through faulty trade treaties, redo the tax structure, at least cut the corporate tax rate, work out a way for corporations to bring back to the US the billions sequestered in foreign countries that should be repatriated to the US so it can be used here, update the military and its equipment, and of course begin work on the infrastructure here at home. Our roads, railroads, and airports need serious maintenance, rehabilitation, and often replacement. Other than by dictat this will take the skills of a super politician-if it is done within the bounds of the constitution—and a master organizer especially since most of these tasks must be done simultaneously.

Meanwhile we are in the midst of the longest bull market ever. Although everything that the government has done over the last decade has had a mediocre effect on improving the US economy, they have done a magnificent job of supporting the investment environment. For the past 2-3 years many analysts and financial gurus have begun to question whether it is time for a major correction or even a severe crash. They claim that most securities are over-valued by many criteria and are riding for a fall. Some are suggesting getting out of stocks and going to gold or bitcoin or other new unregulated currency. Others are taking the other tack, that things will only get better and we will have a 50 year bull market---don't worry, continue to invest and to spend.

I favor a middle of the road approach. No one can reliably predict the movement of the market. All of the systems of the gurus work some of the time but none work all of the time. The safest system that has consistently worked for me through the 1987, the 1999, and the 2008-2010 recessions is reasonable. If you sell too early you will invariably lose out on many opportunities. If you hold on too long and are too optimistic you may lose everything. Through each of the above events I have ended up modestly richer. In the past decade my investment bottom line has about doubled. For the most part, my 30-35% stop loss system has worked. I try to use a trailing stop loss system; i.e., if a stock attains a new high I change the stop loss price such that if it drops by 25% I look at it and if it then drops by

35% below its recent high I sell it.   This means that if stocks are dropping I end up with an amount of cash that allows me to get back in during the recovery.   If I miss the drop by >50%   I consider buying another stake, holding for 30 days and then selling the initial losing shares and taking a tax loss but ending up with more shares. (see pages 77-79.)   If the market is really tanking I consider selling when a stock goes down by 25%, rather than waiting until it achieves a 35% drop.

Getting back in is especially difficult.   The method outlined on pages 145-148 still works and the likelihood of losing is very small.   The key is to maintain sufficient capital so you can begin to reinvest when the turnaround occurs.   There is always a recovery.   The problem is that it is usually in stocks that were not the favorites in the first runup.   Many of these prior favorite stocks may never recover especially if they discontinued or markedly lowered their dividend. The newsletters once again should be your guide, especially Band, Oxford Communique, Skousen, Perry, Spetrino and Leeb.   As a rule they are conservative but have a good eye to recognize when and where to jump in again.   Make sure, however, that you take losses (by doubling up on losers you want to keep and sell the losing shares after 30 days).   It is very upsetting to sell stocks that you have kept a long time taking a loss in your portfolio but having to pay capital gains tax because you bought the stocks cheap many years ago.   When getting back in after a bear market is a good time to accumulate large numbers of shares that everyone shuns (during the recent recession I accumulated significant numbers of shares in large banks, BOA, WF, JPMorgan Chase; most recently with the drop in the price of oil, under 50, I have been buying big oil, Exxon, Total, Chevron, and also natural gas shares Chesapeake, and Cheniere Energy, for cheap.)   Electric cars may eventually win out and wind and solar may beat out gas and oil but there will probably be another runup in these shares before that happens.   When the super bear market appears to be occurring make sure the stocks you hold pay a good dividend, i.e., 4-6 %.   Dividend paying stocks usually recover and will be the first to recover.   Band and Leeb will steer you away from stocks where the dividend is at risk.

Meanwhile with ideas and plans ready for (if) and when the bear takes over, continue to be fully invested following the " best buy" suggestions of the current newsletters (but observing your planned stops) and continue to ride the wave.   Most everything that is predicted will probably occur but the timing remains up in the air and the occurrence of bad times may be postponed for a long time.   Meticulous following and acting on your stops will guarantee that yours losses will be modest and your risk of missing opportunities will be nil.

Epilogue

In summary, pay for good advice via a newsletter and follow the advice.

Reread the chapter on Bad Advice and the summary in the beginning; especially use discipline to cut losses and preserve capital.

Reread the last half of the second addendum chapter with suggestions on what to do now in these economically turbulent times.   Don't be afraid to invest,--- with sense.

If you follow this advice, I expect that you will do surprisingly well.

Time is on your side--- the United States will have good and bad times for the market.   To maintain growth, the government will continue to try to guarantee inflation, hopefully at a modest rate, and investment in companies that will be in business in ten years (that are suggested in the newsletters) will invariably lead to moderate (or great) affluence.

(I won't wish you good luck--- because luck has little to do with it)

JI Haft MD

Other Books by Jacob I. Haft M.D.

Haft JI.: Successful Investing Made Easy. Strategic Book Group, Durham CT, 2011. Actually the second edition of "A Physician's Prescription for Successful Investing."

Haft JI, with Fiks E: The Quick and Easy Heart Book. Everything You Need to Know about Cardiac Health and Operations and What to do after a Heart Attack.   Xlibris Philadelphia, 2005.*

Haft JI: Subduing the Dragon; Living Through a Heart Attack. A Simplified Textbook of Cardiology and Heart Attack. Xlibris, Philadelphia, 2002.*

Haft JI, Karliner JS: Receptor Science in Cardiology. Futura Publishing Company, Mount Kisco, 1984.

Haft JI, Bailey CP(ed.): Advances in the Management of Clinical Heart Disease, Volume IV, Differential Diagnosis of Chest Pain and Other Cardiac Symptoms. Futura Publishing Company, Mount Kisco, 1980.

Haft JI, Berlin S: Consultations with a Cardiologist, Coronary Artery Disease, Volume I, Prevention. Nelson Hall, Chicago, 1979.*

Haft JI, Berlin S: Consultations with a Cardiologist, Coronary Artery Disease, Volume II, Management. Nelson Hall, Chicago, 1979.*

Haft JI, Horowitz M: <u>Clinical Echocardiography.</u> Futura Publishing Company, Mount Kisco, 1978.

Haft JI, Bailey CP(ed.): <u> Advances in the Management of Clinical Heart Disease, Volume III, Therapeutics, Hypertension and Aspects of Echocardiography</u>. Futura Publishing Company, Mount Kisco, l978.

Haft JI, Bailey CP(ed.): <u>Advances in the Management of Clinical Heart Disease. Volume II,Acute Myocadial Infarction and Coronary Artery Disease</u>. Futura Publishing Company, Mount Kisco, 1978.

Haft JI, Bailey CP(ed.): <u>Advances in the Management of Clinical Heart Disease, Volume I.</u> Futura Publishing Company, Mount Kisco,1976.

Donoso E, Haft JI(ed.): <u>Platelets, Thrombosis, Anticoagulation and Acetylsalicylic Acid.</u> Stratton Intercontinental Medical Book Corporation, New York. 1976.

• For laymen.

•

PAPERS:

●

● 1.. Haft JI, Braverman L: Bilateral lymphoepithelioma of the tonsil. NEJM 271:199, 1964.

●

● 2. Kosowsky BD, Stein E, Lau SH, Lister JW, Haft JI, Damato AN:A comparison of the hemodynamic effects of tachycardia produced by atrial pacing and atropine. Am Heart J 72:594, 1966

● 3. Lau SH, Stein E, Kosowsky BD, Haft JI, Lister JW, Damato AN: Atrial pacing and atrioventricular conduction in anomalous atrioventricular excitation (Wolff-Parkinson-White Syndrome). Am J Cardiol 19:354-59, 1967

● 4. Cohen SI, Lau SH, Haft JI, Damato AN: An esophageal electrode for recording arrhythmias. JAMA 200:901, 1967

● 5. Haft JI, Kosowsky BD, Lau SH, Stein E, Damato AN: Termination of atrial flutter by rapid electrical pacing of the atrium. Am J Cardiol 20:239-44, 1967

● 6. Cohen SI, Lau SH, Haft JI, Damato AN: Experimental production of aberrant ventricular conduction in man. Circulation 36:673-85, 1967

● 7. Haft JI, Lau SH, Stein E, Kosowsky BD, Damato AN: Atrial fibrillation produced by atrial stimulation. Circulation 37:70-74, 1968

● 8. Lasser RP, Haft JI, Friedberg CK: Relationship of right bundle branch block and marked left axis deviation (with left parietal or peri-infarction block) to complete heart block and syncope. Circulation 37:429-37, 1968

● 9. Cohen SI, Young MW, Lau SH, Haft JI, Damato AN: Effects of reserpine therapy on cardiac output and atrioventricular conduction during rest and controlled heart rates in patients with essential hypertension. Circulation 37:738-41, 1968

● 10. Kosowsky BD, Haft JI, Lau SH, Stein E, Damato AN: The effects of digitalis on atrioventricular conduction in man. Am Heart J 75:736-741, 19681

● 11. Lau SH, Cohen SI, Stein E, Haft JI, Kinney M, Young M, Helfant R, Damato A: Controlled heart rates by atrial pacing in angina pectoris: a determinant of electrocardiographic ST depression. Circulation 38:711-20, 1968

- 12. Damato AN, Lau SH, Stein E, Haft JI, Kosowsky B, Cohen SI: Cardiovascular response to acute thermal stress (hot dry environment) in unacclimated normal subjects. Am Heart J 76:769-74, 1968

13. Haft JI, Damato AN: Measurement of collateral blood flow, after myocardial infarction in the closed-chest dog. Am Heart J 77:641-48, 1969
- 14. Cannon PJ, Haft JI, Johnson OM: Visual assessment of regional myocardial perfusion utilizing radioactive Xenon-133 and scintillation photography. Circulation 40:277-88, 1969
- 15. Lau SH, Cohen SI, Stein E, Haft JI, Rosen KM, Damato AN: P waves and P loops in coronary sinus and left atrial rhythms. Am Heart J 79:201-14, 1970
- 16. Helfant RH, Forrester JS, Hampton JR, Haft JI, Kemp HG, Gorlin R: Coronary Heart Disease: Differential Hemodynamics, Metabolic and Electrocardiographic effects in patients with and without angina pectoris during atrial pacing. Circulation 42:601, 1970
- 17.   Young BK, Haft JI: Treatment of pulmonary edema with ethacrynic acid during labor. Am J Obst & Gyn 107:330, 1970
- 18. Scherlag B, Helfant RH, Haft JI: Electrophysiology underlying ventricular arrhythmias due to coronary ligation. Am J Physiology 219:1665, 1970
- 19. Johnson PM, Cannon PJ, Haft JI: Scintiphotography of regional myocardial blood flow in the normal and infarcted heart. Amer J Roentgenology 108:708-15, April 1970
- 20. Cohen SI, Lau SH, Haft JI: The intensity of the first heart sound in the Wolff-Parkinson-White Syndrome. Mt. Sinai J of Med 37:17-22, 1971
- 21. Haft JI, Herman MV, Gorlin R: Left bundle branch block: Etiologic hemodynamic and ventriculographic considerations. Circulation 43:279-87, 1971
- 22. Haft JI: Editorial: Assessment of functional significance of coronary artery lesions. Am J Cardiol 27:331-32, 1971
- 23.   Weinstock M, DeGuia R, Daniell M, Haft JI: Inhibition of transvenous pacing through the coronary sinus by the atrial P wave: Diagnosis with the aid of isoproterenol. Chest 59:563-66, May 1971
- 24. Haft JI, Weinstock M, DeGuia R, Gupta PK, Fano A: Assessment of atrioventricular conduction in bilateral bundle branch block and left bundle branch block using HIS bundle electrograms and atrial pacing. Am J Cardiol 27(5):474-80, May 1971
- 25. Haft JI, Weinstock M, DeGuia R: Electrophysiological studies in Mobitz Type 11 second degree heart block. Am J Cardiol 27:682-86, June 1971
- 26. Malsky SJ, Roswit B, Reid CB, Haft JI: Radiation exposure to personnel during cardiac catheterization: A preliminary study. Radiology 100:671-74, 1971
- 27. Lasser RP, Haft JI, Newman BJ, Allen DF, Ishigura J, Friedberg CK: Chronic left heart failure - An experimental model in the dog. Mt. Sinai J of Med 38:440-49, Sept-Oct 1971
- 28. Steiner C, Lau S, Stein E, Wit A, Weiss M, Damato AN, Haft JI, Weinstock M, Gupta P: Electrophysiological documentation of trifascicular block as the common cause of complete heart block. Am J Cardiol 28:436-41, October 1971

- 29. Gupta PK, Haft JI: Complete heart block complicating cardiac catheterization. Chest 61:185-87, February 1972
- 30. Gershengorn K, Haft JI: Intermittent heart block related to treatment of hypertension in a patient with acute myocardial infarction. Chest 61:402-4, April 1972
- 31. Gupta PK, Haft JI: Retrograde Ventriculo-Atrial conduction during complete heart block: Studies with HIS bundle electrography. Amer J Cardiol 30:408, 1972
- 32.   Haft JI, Lasser RP: Electrocardiographic patterns useful in the diagnosis of intermittent heart block. JAMA 22:184, 1972
- 33. Haft JI, Gupta PK, Weinstock M, DeGuia R, Fano A: Effectiveness of small, increasing doses of intramuscular reserpine in hypertension. Chest 62:188, 1972
- 34.   Pasternac A, Gorlin R, Sonnenblick EH, Haft JI, Kempt HG: Abnormalities of ventricular motion induced with pacing in coronary artery disease. Circulation 45:1195-1205, June 1972
- 35.   Haft JI, Kranz PD, Albert FJ, Fani K: Intravascular platelet aggregation in the heart induced by norepinephrine: Electronmicroscopic studies. Circulation 46:698, 1972
- 36. Haft JI, Gershengorn K, Kranz PD, Oestreicher R: Protection against epinephrine induced myocardial necrosis by drugs that inhibit platelet aggregation. Am J Cardiol 30:838, 1972
- 37. Rose H, Kranz P, Weinstock M, Juliano J, Haft JI: Inheritance of combined hyperlipidemia: Evidence for a new lipoprotein phenotype. Am J Med 54:148-60, 1973
- 38.   Haft JI, Fani K: Intravascular platelet aggregation in the heart induced by stress.   Circulation 47:353, 1973
- 39. Haft JI, Kranz PD: Intraventricular conduction intervals during orthograde conduction in patients with complete heart block. Chest 63:751, 1973
- 40. Haft JI, Fano A, Shahabadi A: Clinical experience with Quabain administered in small divided doses in the monitored patient. Chest 63:868, 1973
- 41.   Haft JI: The HIS bundle electrogram, A review. Circulation 47:893-911, 1973
- 42. Haft JI, Kranz PD, Albert F, Oestreicher R: Protective effect of clofibrate against epinephrine induced myocardial necrosis. Am Heart J 86:805-10, 1973
- 43. Haft JI, Levites R: The effects of premature ventricular contractions on AV conduction. Am J of Cardiol 32:794, 1973
- 44. Haft JI, Fani K: Stress and the induction of intravascular platelet aggregation in the heart. Circulation 48:164, 1973
- 45. Haft JI: Treatment of arrhythmias by intracardiac electrical stimulation. A review. Progress in Cardiovascular Dis 16:539-68, 1974.
- 46. Kranz PD, Haft JI, Venkatachalapathy D, Shahabadi A: The hemodynamic effects of oral alpha-methyldopa in the presence and absence of congestive heart failure. Arch of Int Med 134:478-83, Sept. 1974
- 47. Haft JI: Cardiovascular injury induced by sympathetic catecholamines. Progress in Cardiovascular Disease 17:73, 1974

- 48.   Rose HB, Kranz PD, Weinstock M, Juliano J, Haft JI: Combined hyperlipoproteinemia: Evidence for a new lipoprotein phenotype. Atherosclerosis 20:51-64, 1974
- 49. Levites R, Haft JI: Significance of first degree heart block in bifascicular block. Am J of Cardiol 34:259, 1974
- 50. Friedman H, Gomes JAC, Tardio A, Levites R, Haft JI: Appearance of atrial
- rhythm with absent P waves in long standing atrial fibrillation. Chest 66:172, 1974
- 51. Weinstock M, Haft JI: Effect of illness on employment opportunities. AMA Arch of Environ Health 29:79, 1974
- 52. Friedman HS, Gomes JAC, Tardio A, Haft JI: The electrocardiographic features of acute cardiac tamponade. Circulation 50:260, 1974
- 53. Sakurai H, Ackad A, Friedman HS, Haft JI: Aorto-coronary bypass graft surgery in a patient in home dialysis. Clin Neph 2:208-10, 1974
- 54. Haft JI: Quabain: Clinical experience. In "Drugs in Cardiology - Part 2". Edited by E. Donoso. Stratton Intercontinental Medical Book Corp, New York 1975
- 55. Levites R, Haft JI: Evidence suggesting dual A-V nodal pathways in patients without supraventricular tachycardias. Chest 67:36, 1975
- 56. Gomes JAC, Haft JI: WPW Syndrome Type B with HIS depolarization occurring after the QRS: Further evidence that WPW QRS is a fusion beat. Chest 67:445, 1975
- 57. Friedman HS, Gomes JAC, Haft JI: An analysis of Wenckebach periodicity. J Electrocardiology 8:307, 1975
- 58. Levites R, Haft JI: Effects of exercise-induced stress on platelet aggregation. Cardiology 60:304, 1975
- 59. Haft JI: Effect of stress on platelet aggregation in the heart. In "Cardiovascular Problems, Perspective and Progress". Edited by Henry I. Russeck, 1976, p. 251-62
- 60. Haft JI, Gomes JAC: The Wolff-Parkinson-White Syndrome. The value of the HIS bundle electrogram. Catheterization and Cardiovascular Diagnosis 2:113, 1976
- 61.   Levites R, Toor M, Haft JI: Progressive improvement in His-Purkinje conduction during recovery from catheter-induced heart block. Am Heart J 91:79, 1976
- 62. Haft JI, Arkel YS: Effect of emotional stress on platelet aggregation in humans. Chest 70:501, 1976
- 63. Gomes JAC, Venkatachalapathy D, Haft JI: The effect of Vitamin E on platelet aggregation. Am Heart J 91:425-29, 1976
- 64. Levites R, Haft JI, Calderon J, Venkatachalapathy D: Effects of procainamide on the dispersion of recovery of excitability during coronary occulsion. Circulation 53:982-84, 1976
- 65. Levites R, Haft JI: Effects of lidocaine on intramyocardial conduction in non-ischemic and ischemic canine myocardium. Cardiovascular Research 10:687, 1976
- 66. Haft JI: Editorial: The HV interval and patients with bifascicular block. Electrocardiology 10:1, 1977
- 67. Levin AR, Haft JI, Engle MA, Ehler KH, Klein AA: Intracardiac conduction intervals in children with congenital heart disease. Comparison of HIS bundle studies

in 42 normal children and 307 patients with congenital cardiac defects. Circulation 55:286, 1977

- 68. Haft JI: Clinical indications for the HIS bundle electrogram. Cardiovascular Medicine 2:449, 1977
- 69. Haft JI: Clinical implications of atrioventricular and intraventricular conduction defects. I. In "Clinical-Electrocardiographic Correlations". Edited by JC Rios, FA Davis,   Philadelphia, PA, 1977, p. 25-40
- 70. Haft JI: Clinical implications of atrioventricular and intraventricular conduction defects. II. Acute myocardial infarction. Ibid, p. 41-64, 1977
- 71. Gomes JAC, Haft JI: HIS bundle electrocardiography in the Wolff-Parkinson-White Syndrome. Evidence for combination of a James and Mahaim Conduction. Cardiology 62:355, 1977
- 72. Arkel YS, Haft JI, Kreutner W, Sherwood J, Williams R: Alteration in second phase platelet aggregation associated with an emotionally stressful activity. Thrombosis and Haemostasis 38:552, 1977
- 73. Schiller MD, Levin AR, Haft JI, Engle MA, Ehlers KH, Klein AA: Electrophysiologic studies in sick sinus syndrome following surgery for D-transposition of the great arteries. J of Peds 91:891, 1977
- 74. Younan KY, Haft JI: Reversible anterior Q waves in the absence of myocardial infarction: Myocardial scintigraphic findings. J of Med Soc NJ 75(5):475-78, 1978
- 75. Arkel YS, Haft JI, Williams R: Alteration in second phase platelet aggregation associated with emotionally stressful activity in "Platelet Function Testing". DHEW Pub. No. (NIH) 78-1087, p. 705-17, 1978
- 76. Friedman HS, Zaman Q, Haft JI, Melendez S: Assessment of atrioventricular conduction in aortic valve disease. British Heart J 40:911, 1978
- 77. Haft JI: Current status of anti-platelet therapy. ACCEL. Vol. II, No. 1, Jan. 1979
- 78. Haft JI: The role of blood platelets in coronary artery disease. Am J Cardiol 43:1197-1206, 1979
- 79. Gutman JA, Haft JI: Chronic chest pain and dyspnea caused by occult constrictive pericarditis. J Med Soc of NJ 76:517-20, 1979
- 80. Gutman JA, Haft JI: Mediastinal tumor presenting as a new heart murmur. J Med Soc of NJ 76:364-66. 1979
- 81. Haft JI: Platelets and coronary artery disease. Primary Cardiology 5:97-104, 1979
- 82. Haft JI, Gonnella GR, Kirtane JS, Anastasiades A: Correlations of the ear crease sign with coronary arteriographic findings. Cardiovascular Medicine 4:861-67, 1979
- 83. Schiller MS, Levin AR, Haft JI, Klein AA, Ehlers KH, Engle MA: Electrophysiologic studies in a child with concealed preexcitation syndrome. Cardiovascular Medicine 4(3):345-52, March 1979
- 84. Gutman JA, Haft JI: Atrial fibrillation in the Wolff-Parkinson White Syndrome. J of Med Soc of NJ 76(13):907-12, 1979
- 85.   Haft JI, Pellicano JF, Prior M: Clinical and conceptual implications of coronary arteriographic findings in patients with anterior myocardial infarction. Excerpta Medica International Congress Series 491:406-9, 1980.

- 86.   Timins BI, Gutman JA, Haft JI: Diisopyramide induces heart block. Chest 79:472-79, 1981
- 87. Haft JI: Catecholamines, stress, platelets and coronary artery disease. In "Platelets in Cardiovascular Disease". Edited by J. Mehta. Futura, Mt. Kisco, New York 265-77, 1981
- 88. Foerster JM, Haft JI, Parmley WM, Russell RO, Norman FW, Bulger JJ: Investigating clues to acute MI; testing the evidence of acute MI. Patient Care 15, 15:22-85, Nov. 15, 1981
- 89. Agarwal SK, Haft JI: The atrial repolarization wave and spurious ST segment abnormalities. J of Med Soc of NJ 79:315-16, 1982
- 90. Agarwal SK, Malhotra S, Haft JI: Severe aortic regurgitation - an echocardiographic diagnosis. Arch Int Med 142:1625, 1982
- 91. Haft JI, Bachik M: Progression of coronary artery disease in patients with chest pain and normal or intraluminal disease on arteriography. Am Heart J 107:35-39, 1982
- 92. Arkel YS, Haft JI, Buxton M, Herbert S, Burghardt C, Williams R: Emotional arousal and platelet physiology: A review and some original contributions. J of Human Stress 19-27, 1982
- 93. Agarwal SK, Haft JI: Flail mitral leaflet: An echocardiographic diagnosis. J of Med Soc of NJ 79:404-08, 1982
- 94. Foerster JM, Haft JI, Parmley WM, Russell RO, Norman FW, Bulger JJ: Acute MI: Steps toward stabilization. Patient Care 16, 19:15-65, Nov. 15, 1982
- 95. Agarwal SK, Haft JI: Exit Block. J Nat Med Assoc 74:1026-8, 1982
- 96. Foerster JM, Haft JI, Parmley WM, Russell RO, Norman FW, Bulger JJ: Acute MI: Treatment of complications. Patient Care 17, 5:91-131, Feb. 15, 1983
- 97. Bachik M, Agarwal SK, Haft JI: Idiopathic hypertrophic subaortic stenosis and acute myocardial infarction. An uncommon association. J Nat Med Assoc 75:305-309, 1983
- 98.   Haft JI, DeMaio SJ, Bartoszyk OB: Coronary arteriographic findings in symptomatic right bundle branch block. Am J Cardiology 53:770-73, 1984
- 99. Agarwal SK, Haft JI, Bachik M: Case report: Aneurysm of the descending aorta. NJ J of Med 81:211-13, 1984
- 100.   Agarwal SK, Haft JI, Goldstein JE: Postmyocardial infarction rupture of the ventricular septum. J Med Soc of NJ 81:110-12, 1984
- 101.   Haft JI, Litterer WE: Chewing nifedipine to rapidly treat hypertension. Arch of Int Med 12:2357-59, 1984
- 102.   DeGregorio B, Goldstein JE, Haft JI: Administration of intracoronary streptokinase during menstruation. Am Heart J 109:908-10, 1985
- 103.   Ambrose JA, Winters SL, Arora RR, Haft JI, Goldstein JE, Rentrop KP, Gorlin R, Fuster V: Coronary angiographic morphology in myocardial infarction: A link between the pathogenesis of unstable angina and myocardial infarction. JACC 6:1233-8, 1985
- 104.   Haft JI: Use of calcium-channel blocker nifedipine in the management of hypertension emergency. Amer J Emergency Med Suppl. 3(6):25, Dec. 1985

- 105.   Niemiera MI, Haft JI, Goldstein JE, Hobson RW: Retrograde internal mammary artery flow and resistant angina pectoris: Clue to the coronary-subclavian steal syndrome. Catheterization and Diagnosis 12:93-95, 1986
- 106.   Haft JI, Habbab MA: Effectiveness of IV verapamil preceded by calcium chloride in the treatment of atrial arrhythmias. Arch of Int Med 146:1085, 1986
- 107.   Habbab MA, Szwed SA, Haft JI: Is coronary arterial spasm part of the aspirin-induced asthma syndrome? Chest 90:141-143, 1986
- 108.   Habbab MA, Haft JI: Intravenous nitroglycerin in heparin resistance. Ann Int Med 105:305, Aug. 1986
- 109.   Habbab MA, Goldstein JE, Haft JI: Intravenous streptokinase and percutaneous intraaortic balloon counterpulsation used concomitantly. Am Heart J 113:205-207, Jan. 1987
- 110.   Angeli SA, Haft JI: Severe coronary artery disease in a marathon runner. Chest 91:271-72, Feb. 1987
- 111.   Habbab MA, Haft JI: Characteristic pulsed Doppler findings in patients with flail mitral valve. Chest 91:571-75, April 1987
- 112.   Habbab MA, Haft JI: Heparin resistance induced by intravenous nitroglycerin. Arch Int Med 147:857-60, May 1987
- 113.   Habbab MA, Senft AG, Haft JI: Origin of the right coronary artery from the left anterior descending coronary artery: A very rare anomaly of coronary arterial origin. Am Heart J 114:169-70 July 1987
- 114.   Haft JI, Niemiera M: The coronary arteriographic lesion of unstable angina. Chest 92:609-12, 1987
- 115.   Angeli SA, Haft JI: Noninvasive determination of cardiac output in patient with mitral stenosis using echocardiographic and Doppler data,. J of Cardiovascular Ultrasonography 6:323-29, Dec. 1987
- 116.   Haft JI, Goldstein JE, DeGregorio B: Aortic valve balloon dilatation: Non-operative treatment of aortic stenosis. NJ Med 84(12):863-66, 1987
- 117.   Haft JI, Altieri JJ, Smith LG, Herskowitz M: Computerized axial tomography of the abdomen in the diagnosis of splenic emboli. Arch of Int Med 148:193-97, Jan. 1988
- 118.   Goulah RD, Goldstein JE, Haft JI: Salvage PTCA in patient who ware not candidates for coronary surgery. NJ Med 85:223-25, March 1988
- 119.   Goulah RD, Rose MR, Strober M, Haft JI: Coronary dissection following trauma with systemic emboli. Chest 93:887-8, April 1988
- 120.   Haik BJ, Haft JI: Coronary artery disease in a young woman with SLE. NJ Med 85:295-97, April 1988
- 121.   Haft JI: Catastrophic progression in coronary artery disease. Cardio 5(7):62-64, July 1988
- 122.   Haft JI, Haik BJ, Goldstein JE, Brodyn N: Development of significant coronary artery lesions in areas of minimal disease. A common mechanism for coronary disease progression. Chest, Oct. 1988
- 123.   Haft JI, Goldstein JE, Altieri JJ, Schnomuller A: Combined percutaneous aortic valvuloplasty and percutaneous coronary angioplasty. NJ Med 85:815-17, Oct. 1988

- 124.   Haft JI, Adami JL: Thallium stress testing and left bundle branch block. Contemporary Internal Medicine, April 1989, p. 44-47
- 125.   Haft JI, Bassil H, Goldstein JE, Haik BJ: Morphology of coronary lesions in the prediction of early PTCA outcome. Catheterization and Cardiovascular Diagnosis 17:69-74, May 1989
- 126.   Tabbalat R, Haft JI: Left atrial myxoma. NJ Med 86:785-88, Oct. 1989
- 127.   Adami JL, Haft JI: Treating unstable angina with PTCA. Contemporary Internal   Medicine, June 1989, p. 43-45
- 128.   Haft JI: Essential equipment for hemodynamic monitoring in a small hospital. J of Critical Illness 4(4):14, April 1989
- 129.   Goulah RP, Goldstein JE, Haft JI: PTCA in anomalous coronary artery. NJ Med 86(7):548-50, July 1989
- 130.   Brodyn NE, Goldstein JE, Haft JI: Valvuloplasty for mitral and aortic stenosis. Contemporary Internal Medicine, Sept. 1989, pp 50-55
- 131.   Haft JI: Morphology of coronary artery lesions: Important insights into pathogenesis of ischemic coronary syndromes. J of St. Michael's Med Ctr 1:19-24, 1989
- 132.   Al-Zarka A, Haft JI: Use of tissue plasminogen activator in the Coronary Care Unit for acute closure after coronary angioplasty. Chest 95(5):1241-42, May 1990
- 133.   Brodyn NE, Rose MR, Prior FP, Haft JI: Left atrial diastolic compression in a patient with a large pericardial effusion and pulmonary hypertension. Am J of Med 88(1):65-66, Jan. 1990
- 134.   Adami JL, Haft JI: PTCA following acute MI and thrombolysis. Contemporary Internal Medicine 2(2):56 Feb. 1990
- 135.   Rubenstein DG, Haft JI: Combining CABG with automatic implantable cardioverter/defibrillator. Contemporary Internal Medicine, May 1990
- 136.   Homoud MK, Aaronoff M, Goldstein JE, Haft JI: PTCA following myocardial infarction: Use of bailout fibrinolysis to improve results. Am Heart J 120:243-47, Aug. 1990
- 137.   Homoud MK, Haft JI: Prothetic mitral valve dysfunction presenting as syncope. Contemporary Int Med 2(8): 66-70, Sept. 1990
- 138.   Rubenstein DG, Haft JI: Cardiac electrophysiological studies: Their indications and clinical value. J of St. Michael's Med Ctr Vol. 2, #1 Fall/Winter 1990
- 139.   Tabbalat R, Haft JI: Coronary angioplasty in symptomatic patients after bypass surgery. Am Heart J 120:1091:96, Nov. 1990
- 140.   Santana J, Haft JI: Recurrent angina following PTCA. Contemporary Int Med   November/December 1990, p. 84-86
- 141.   Al-Zarka AM, Haft JI, Bassil HF, Goldstein JE, Arkel YS, Lake-Lewin D: Correlation of Cross-linked Fibrin Degradation Products (D-Dimer) with coronary angiographic lesion morphology. Intl J of Cardiology 30:77-87, Jan. 1991
- 142.   Tabbalat RA, H aft JI: Effect of severe pulmonary hypertension on the calculation of mitral valve area in patients with mitral stenosis. Am Heart J 121:488-93, Feb. 1991

- 143. Haft JI, Al-Zarka AM: Origin and fate of complex coronary lesions. Am Heart J 121:1050-61, 1991
- 144. Tabbalat RA, Haft JI, Homoud MK: Percutaneous balloon valvuloplasty in the treatment of mitral stenosis. J of St. Michael's Med Ctr 3(1):8-13 Spring/Summer 1991
- 145. Christou C, Haft JI: Interventricular septal rupture following MI. Contemporary Int Med. March 1991, p. 49-56
- 146. Homoud M, Goldstein JE, Haft JI: Transluminal atherectomy proves effective. Contemporary Int Med, January 1992, p. 86-91
- 147. Haft JI, Goldstein JE: A "true" left main coronary artery equivalent lesion. Contemporary Int Med, March 1992, p. 80-84
- 148. Santana J, Haft JI, LaMarche NS, Goldstein JE: Coronary angioplasty in patients eighty years of age or older. Am Heart J 124:13-18, 1992
- 149. Mantecon IJ, Haft JI, Rubenstein DG: Radiofrequency ablation cures Wolff-Parkinson-White Syndrome. Contemporary Int Med, Sept. 1992, p. 99-105
- 150. Tabbalat RA, Haft JI: Are reciprocal changes a consequence of "ischemia at a distance" or merely a benign electrical phenomenon: A PTCA study. Am Heart J 126:95-103, 1993
- 151. Vehra I, Haft JI, Khalighi K, Kelly M: Using a thallium scan to predict myocardial viability. Contemporary Int Med 5(6):80-82, 1993
- 152. Haft JI, Al-Zarka AM: Comparison of the natural history of irregular and smooth coronary lesions: Insights into the pathogenesis, progression and prognosis of coronary atherosclerosis. Am Heart J 126:551-61, 1993
- 153. Tonnessen GE, Haft JI, Rubenstein DG: Clinical value of signal-averaged ECG: Its correlation with induction of ventricular tachycardia. J of St. Michael's Med Ctr 5(1):5-8, 1993
- 154. Sanchez R, Haft JI: Temporal relationship of complications post coronary artery bypass graft surgery: Scheduling for safe discharge. Am Heart J 127:282-6, 1994
- 155. Weinberg H, Haft JI: Atrial fibrillation signals left ventricular dysfunction. Contemporary Int Med 6(1):10-11, Jan. 1994
- 156. Amsterdam EA, Chatterjee K, Haft JI, Hochman J, Scarpinato L: Heading off trouble in unstable angina. Patient Care 28(10):12-31, May 1994
- 157. Tonnessen GE, Haft JI, Fulton J, Rubenstein DG: Value of tilt table testing with isoproterenol in determining therapy in adults with syncope and pre-syncope of unexplained origin. Arch Int Med 154(14):1613-17, July 25, 1994
- 158. Khalighi K, Tullo NG, Haft JI: Catheter ablation of the slow AV nodal pathway in AV nodal re-entry tachycardia. NJ Med 91(2):103-6, 1994
- 159. Chatterjee K, Haft JI, Hochman J, Scarpinato L: Rising to the challenge of acute MI. Patient Care 28(12):126-38, July 1994
- 160. Kanu C, Haft JI, Hochman J, Scarpinato L: Gaining ground on cardiogenic shock. Patient Care 28(15):24-38, 1994
- 161. Khalighi K, Haft JI: Adenosine in the diagnosis of wide complex tachycardias. Contemporary Int Med 6(12):40-43, 1994

- 162. Haft JI, Hammoudeh AJ, Cont PJ: Assessing myocardial viability: Correlation of myocardial wall motion abnormalities and pathological Q waves with technetium-99m sestamibi single-photon emission computed tomography. Am Heart J 130(5):994-998, Nov. 1995
- 163. Haft JI, Christou CP, Goldstein JE, Carnes RE: Correlation of atherectomy specimen histology with coronary arteriographic lesion morphologic appearance in patients with stable and unstable angina. Am Heart J 130(3 Part 1):420-24, Sept.1995
- 164. Khalighi K, Haft JI, Vehra I: Intraluminal balloon dilation for coarctation of the aorta. Contemporary Int Med 8(1):84-87, Jan. 1996
- 165. Khalighi K, Haft JI, Goldstein JE: Second procedures: Selecting the best option for your patient. Contemporary Int Med 8(6):82-84, June 1996166. Hammoudeh AJ, Haft JI, Eichman GT: Hemoptysis and unilateral intra-alveolar hemorrhage complicating intravenous thrombolysis for myocardial infarction. Clinical Cardiology 19:595-96, July 1996
- 167. Haft JI, Christou CP, Goldstein JE, Carnes RE: Atherectomy and complex coronary lesions. Pg. 73-78. In "Complex Coronary Lesions in Acute Coronary Syndromes". Edited by JA Ambrose. Future Publishing Co, Inc., Armonk, NY, 1996
- 168. Hammoudeh AJ, Haft JI: Coronary-plaque rupture in acute coronary syndromes triggered by snow shoveling. NEJM 335(26):2001, Dec. 26, 1996
- 169. Hammoudeh AJ, Haft JI: Optimizing cardiac risk related to non-cardiac vascular surgery. Contemporary Int Med Vol. 8, #12, Dec. 1996
- 170. Haft JI, Mariano DL, Goldstein JE: Comparison of the histopathology of culprit lesions in chronic stable angina, unstable angina, and myocardial infarction. Clinical Cardiology 20:651-55, 1997
- 171. Saadeh SA, Haft JI: Correlation of troponin T levels with ruptured plaques. NEJM 336:1257, April 14, 1997
- 172 Shamoon FE, Goldstein JE, Haft JI: Restoration of patency of left internal mammary artery graft with progression of the underlying left anterior descending coronary artery disease. Catheterization and Cardiovascular Diagnosis 42:213-15, 1997
- 173. Haft JI, Hammoudeh AJ: More on coronary-plaque rupture triggered by snow shoveling. NEJM Correspondence 336:1678-79, June 1997
- 174. Chakhtoura EY, Shamoon FE, Haft JI, Obiedzinski GR, Cohen AJ, Watson RM: Comparison of platelet activation in unstable and stable angina pectoris and correlation with coronary angiographic findings. American Journal of Cardiology 2000 Aug 15;86(8):835-839
- 175. Haft JI: Multiple atherosclerotic plaque rupture in acute coronary syndrome. Circulation. 2003 Mar 11;107(9); e65-6
- 176. Amato JL, Shamoon FE, Haft JI: Thrombus aspiration during primary percutaneous coronary intervention. NEJM 2008 Jun 12;358(24);2640
- 177. Haft JI: Echocardiographic findings that may help identify occult intermittent atrial fibrillation in hypertensive patients at risk for a second (or first) stroke. Stroke. 2008 Jun;39(6): e91

- 178.   Haft JI, Teichholz LE: Echocardiographic and clinical risk factors for atrial fibrillation in hypertensive patients with ischemic stroke. Am J Cardiol. 2008 Nov 14;102(10):1348-5
- 179   Haft JI: Using CHADS2 backwards plus echo criteria to identify stroke patients who have occult atrial fibrillation. Am Heart J 2009 Feb; 157(2):e9. doi:10.1016/j.ahj 2008,10.014. Epub 2008 Dec 19.
- 180.   Haft JI: Continuum of cognitive impairment to stroke possibly via atrial fibrillation. Ann Neulol. 2011 Oct;70 (4):666-7
- 181.   Amato JL Jr, Haft JI: Subclinical atrial fibrillation and the risk of stroke. N Engl J Med. 2012 Apr 5;366(14):1351.
- 182.   Haft JI: The importance of atrial fibrillation/flutter as a cause of ischemic stroke..Int j Cardiol. 2012 Jun 28;158(1):143-4.
- 183.   Gupta N, Haft JI, Bajaj S, Samuel A, Parikh R, Pandya, D, Shamoon F. Role of the combined CHADS2 score and echocardiographic abnormalities in predicting stroke in patients with proxysmal atrial fibrillation. J Clin Neurosci. 2012 Sep; 19(9):1242-5.
- 184.   Haft JI: Stroke prevention in atrial fibrillation: impact of novel oral anticoagulants. Clin Appl Thromb Hemost. 2013 Jun; 19(3):241-8.
- 185.   Haft JI, Teichholz LE: High incidence of atrial fibrillation or flutter in stroke patients who have the clinical risk factors for stroke. Journal of Atrial Fibrillation. 2013 Aug-Sep Vol 6 Issue 2, pg 114-119.
- 186.   Haft JI, Teichholz LE: Clinical heart failure patients with ischemic stroke have a high incidence (>60%) of atrial fibrillation or flutter whether systolic function is preserved or depressed. World Journal of Cardiovascular Diseases. 2014; 4:455-464. http://dx.doi.org/10.4236/wjcd.2014.49055
- 187.   Haft JI: Letter by Haft regarding article,"High prevalence of atrial fibrillation among patients with ischemic stroke". Stroke.2015;46:e11
- 188.   Haft JI: Letter by Haft regarding article,"Temporal relationship between subclinial atrial fibrillation and embolic events." Circulation. 2015;131:e337-e338.

Internet Addresses

Favorites:

John Dessauer: www.johndessauerinvestments.com

Stephen Leeb; Complete Investor: www.completeinvestor.com

Richard E. Band; Profitable Investing: www.rband.com

Richard C. Young; Intelligence Report: www.intelligencereport.com

Louis Navalier; Blue Chip Growth: www.navaliergrowth.investorplace.com

Mark Skousen; Forecasts and Strategies:www.MarkSkousen.com

Oxford Club; Communique: www.oxfordclub.com

Richard Maroney; Dow Theory Forecasts: www.DowTheory.com

Paul Larson: Morningstar Stock Investor: www.morningstar.com

Porter Stansberry; Investment Advisory: www.stansberryresearch.com
   Also at this address: Steve Sjuggerud's True Wealth

Others:

Keith Fitz-Gerald; Money Map Report: www.moneymappress.com
      Also Michael Robinson; Nova X report,   Kent Moors;:Energy Advantage:

Josh Peters; Morningstar Dividend Investor: www.morningstar.com

Bryan Perry; Cash Machihe: www..bryan perryinvesting.com

Bill Spetrino; The Dividend Macine:www.newsmax.com

Nathan Slaughter; High Yield Investing:www.streetauthority.com
:
Louis Basenese;True Alpha:www.agorafinancial.com
   Also Technology Profits Confidential

Richard Moroney; Upside:www.upsidestocks.com

Motley Fool Stock Advisor:www.fool.com/premium/stock-advisor/

Royden Ward; Benjamin Graham,Value Letter:www.cabotwealth.com
   Also go to Huff's Cabot Undervalued Stocks Advisor

Teeka Tiwari; Palm Beach Letter:www.palmbeachgroup.com

www.ingramcontent.com/pod-product-compliance
Lightning Source LLC
Chambersburg PA
CBHW032015170526
45157CB00002B/702